Blockbuster Quilts

B118

by Margaret J. Miller

CREDITS

Photography . . . . Brent Kane
Illustration and Graphics . . . . Stephanie Benson
Laurel Strand
Text and Cover Design . . . . Judy Petry
Editors . . . . Liz McGehee
Shellie Tucker

Blockbuster Quilts©
©1991 by Margaret J. Miller
That Patchwork Place, Inc., PO Box 118, Bothell, WA 98041-0118

Printed in the Republic of Korea
98 97 96 95 94 93 92 91   6 5 4 3 2 1

Library of Congress Cataloging-in-Publication Data

Miller, Margaret J.
    Blockbuster quilts / Margaret J. Miller.
        p.   cm.
    ISBN 0-943574-75-7
    1. Quilting—Patterns. I. Title.
TT835.M52 1991
746.9'7—dc20

90-15476
CIP

DEDICATION

To my mother, Isabel Anderson Blackhall, whose love of needlework runs in my veins

And to my father, Arthur Howard Thompson, whose strong belief in what I could make of myself and whose constant encouragement to "stay upbeat" will continue to sustain me all my life

ACKNOWLEDGMENTS

My heartfelt thanks go to:

My husband Paul, who jokes about his handprint in the middle of my back, pushing me along in my career;

My sons, David Andrew Miller and Allen Edward Miller, whose appreciation of the work I do is a gift very much appreciated;

Students in my quiltmaking classes through the years, who have opened my eyes over and over again to the real adventure of quiltmaking, and whose sense of excitement at the prospect of making yet another kind of pieced surface was like coals burning—it took little effort to fan those coals in the flame of creative exhilaration;

Every quiltmaking friend and fellow guild member who has gasped at, applauded, or admired my work, or given me blocks to put together over the years—you all have contributed significantly to my growth as a quiltmaker;

All those individuals and groups that loaned quilts for publication in this book: Ann M. Albertson, Escondido, California; Pamela Anderson, Burlington, Washington; Canyon Quilters Guild, San Diego, California; Betty Charette, Aberdeen, Washington; Rachel Kincy Clark, Watsonville, California; Susan M. Connoley, Gig Harbor, Washington; Marjory Crist, Santa Rosa, California; Jeanne Duncan, Bartlesville, Oklahoma; Friendship Quilters Guild, Poway, California; Evelyn M. Griffin, Puyallup, Washington; Loma Gene Hersom, San Jose, California; Cody Mazuran, Salt Lake City, Utah; Barbara McCroskey, Carmel, Indiana; Sara Quattlebaum, Olympia, Washington; Pat Scoville, Westlake Village, California; Bernice McCoy Stone, Kensington, California; Dr. and Mrs. Arthur Thompson, College Park, Maryland; Martha Williams, Kent, Washington;

Nancy J. Martin and the entire staff at That Patchwork Place for their encouragement and constant support;

My special friends, especially Jeana Kimball, Mary Hickey, and Marion Shelton, who encouraged the writing of this book and said "You can do it" when I needed to hear it most.

Contents

Preface

Reach for the Unexpected" is the theme of this book, which has grown out of my desire that quiltmakers engage in quiltmaking for the sheer adventure of making quilts; to enjoy building on the tradition, using traditional quilt block patterns as a jumping-off place for innovative pieced surface design.

This book is not an attempt to go from traditional to bizarre (which is synonymous with contemporary, in some ways of thinking), but rather to present some innovative ways of assembling old blocks, well-loved patterns, into quilts with a refreshing new look. The goal of this book is to get the reader to think in terms of the entire pieced surface instead of individual blocks, and to begin making quilts whose overall pattern is not predictable after a viewer sees just one block.

Blockbuster Quilts grew out of a series of personal design exercises in which I was given groups of blocks by different people for the purpose of assembling them into an innovative whole. This was always a challenge because I had to work with other people's color choices, with varied sizes and numbers of blocks—mostly, because I had to make a harmonious whole out of a sometimes disparate group of elements.

Since quiltmaking has gone substantially beyond the stage of being a passing craze to being a significant industry in the United States and around the world, students continue to take classes and make blocks, and some of these blocks have not yet found their way into quilt tops. In the thousands of quilt guilds across the country, quiltmakers win groups of blocks; neighborhood friendship groups make blocks for each other; quiltmakers collect favorite patterns in a conglomeration of fabrics from antique shops.

To all quiltmakers who have some long-forgotten blocks in drawers and boxes, this book is for you. So dig out those blocks, and prepare to have some fun! After all, even if the ideas you try with your old blocks don't work out, you will have made progress as a quiltmaker, and the blocks will be much happier for being used instead of left in the closet for the next generation of quiltmakers to discover.

Introduction

This is not meant to be a pattern book, but rather a book of ideas—of design concepts—of jumping-off places for the creation of innovative pieced surfaces. The focus is on reaching for the unexpected in pieced surface design—by changing angles commonly found in traditional patchwork patterns, by camouflaging where one block stops and the next one begins, by concealing where the blocks stop and the border begins, and most important, by keeping the entire pieced surface in mind during the design process.

Therefore, *Blockbuster Quilts* is not a complete guide to the mechanics of making a quilt. There is an appendix presenting the method I use to get from graph-paper design to quilt top, but this is offered as one of several ways to approach quiltmaking.

Though *Blockbuster Quilts* is not a pattern book, the line drawings of quilts which appear in the Putting It All Together chapter will show the reader how some quilts were designed on graph paper.

The focus of the book is quilt design and layout, not color planning, though a brief section explaining color strategies is presented on pages 119–130. Also, the design process is restricted to consideration of straight-line piecing only. Curved seams are beyond this book's scope. However, by changing the angles used in designing blocks and block settings, one can achieve the look of gentle curves even though only straight-line piecing is used.

How to Use This Book

The book's primary chapters concern 1) blocks together, 2) pathways among the blocks, and 3) borders. In each chapter there are subdivisions, and each of these presents a different design mechanism by which you may achieve an unexpected look in a quilt obviously based on traditional patterns. There are design exercises for the reader to try in each subdivision; it is important to do these exercises in order, since many of them build on previous ones. I strongly recommend that the reader peruse the entire book before embarking on design exercises, so as to have the total picture in mind first (much in the way the reader will endeavor to keep the entire quilt surface in mind as the design process progresses).

In the fourth chapter of the book, some guidelines on moving color across the pieced quilt surface are presented. By applying the various color strategies presented there to a single pieced design, the reader can discover new ways of sprinkling color across the quilt. The strategies are shown in both a traditional and a more contemporary block grouping in the form of color mock-ups; these mock-ups are intended to suggest possibilities, not prescribe color choices to the reader.

In the book's fifth chapter, Putting It All Together: The Quilts, many of the quilts presented in color in earlier chapters are diagrammed and described one by one. By studying the line drawings and the color plates

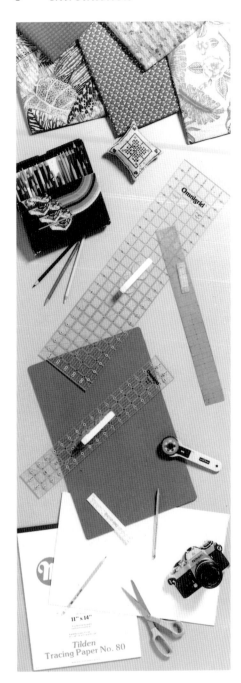

which appear throughout the book, the reader can see how the various design mechanisms discussed may be combined in real quilts.

It is hoped the reader will use this book as an exercise in the adventure of quiltmaking, not as a book of rules delineating "good" and "bad" quilts. Neither is it intended that decision making become more of an agony. Rather, I present this book in the spirit of fun, and aim to simplify the overwhelming number of decisions some quiltmakers try to make all at once.

The quilts that arise from ideas presented in this book are not quilts which can be made overnight. They are quilts that will be memorable for their design, and treasured as such over the years.

Supplies

To work in the **design portion** of the book, you will need:

Graph paper—cross-section pad (which means there is a heavier blue line printed every inch). I recommend eight squares to the inch. Fewer squares to the inch are too large to work in detail; more squares to the inch are too hard to see. Large pad (11" x 17") is recommended.

Tracing paper—a pad large enough to cover the graph paper.

Colored paper—a few sheets; may be construction paper or colored magazine pages.

Rulers—two sizes: 2" x 18" and 1" x 6" (clear plastic rulers with a red grid printed on them are especially useful).

Pencils—your favorites: mechanical with 0.5mm lead, or tried-and-true wooden #2 lead pencils.

Eraser

Rubber cement

Glue stick

Scissors for paper

Good reference book of patchwork patterns (several are listed in the Bibliography, page 167).

Access to a photocopy machine!

Good lighting

Three-ring binder—to house your personal idea book, the result of the discoveries you make through the exercises in this book.

This last item, the idea book, is a crucial tool in your development as a quiltmaker. In the form of one or more large three-ring binders, it serves as an easily organized place to accumulate ideas, drawings, words that inspire you, patterns, notes on quilts you have made in the past, and other important quiltmaking information. This idea book will be a treasure trove of jumping-off places for new quilt designs in the future.

As you keep adding to your idea book over a number of years (it will quickly grow to more than one binder full), it will become valuable as a historical document that records your development as a quiltmaker. The idea book will illustrate how your sense of color develops, and how you tackle increasingly complex projects over the years. Moreover, you may be surprised to discover there the threads of those designs to which you return again and again in your work.

You may want to use a set of index dividers to organize the idea book into sections. Just a few divisions are suggested here (you will come up with other divisions which suit your specific needs and work habits):

Historical Documents

A single descriptive sheet for every quilt you have made, listing date begun and date finished; fabric swatches, perhaps; stories associated with the quilt; prizes it may have won. Include a photograph of the front and back of each quilt, perhaps a closeup photograph of the signature label (or the area of the quilt in which your name and the date of the quilt appear). This section should be kept in a notebook all its own—in an area where it can be retrieved quickly in case of fire in your home or studio.

Originals

Drawings, sketches, ideas for new quilts scribbled on assorted pieces of paper (napkins, grocery receipts, etc.).

Words

Sayings or quotations—about art, quilts, or quiltmakers, for example—that inspire you.

Photographs

These might be from quilt shows, photos of nature that inspire you, color combinations from advertisements that appeal to you, etc.

Templates

Templates may be stored in large manila envelopes which have been three-hole punched to be held in this book. Larger templates may require storage elsewhere, but keeping all templates from each project together facilitates "working in a series" and exploring various color strategies within the same graphic mechanism, your quilt.

Descriptive Divisions (such as those used in this book)

"Blocks Together," "Offset Blocks," "Distorted Blocks," "Color Strategies," and so on.

Storage

Some of the exercises in *Blockbuster Quilts* may involve using tracing and graph paper too large for the idea book. For separate storage of these items, you may wish to use transparent plastic pockets, available from larger art or office supply stores or college bookstores.

To work in the **quiltmaking portion** of this book, you will need:

Sketch of quilt design to scale
Graph paper—a large cross-section pad (17" x 22"). Again, eight squares to the inch are recommended.
Posterboard—from the drugstore or dime store. White or a light color is preferred. Buy the large sheets—22" x 28".
Spray adhesive
Scotch tape
Rubber cement
Scissors for paper
Pencils for marking fabric—#2 lead pencil, #4B lead pencil, and silver colored pencil (don't buy gray color by mistake!).
Rotary cutting equipment—large-wheel rotary cutter; cutting surface for rotary cutter—the larger, the better (mine is 23" x 35"); Plexiglas

straightedges—3" x 18" and 6" x 24" (6" square and 15" square also useful).

Fabrics—firmly woven, good- to high-quality cottons and cotton/polyester blend fabrics recommended (not 100% polyester)

Sewing machine in good working order, and accessories

Iron and ironing surface

Vertical design surface—This is essential to good quilt design analysis. It could consist of: 1) 4' x 8' panel(s) of Celotex or soundboard, covered with flannel fabric, or 2) lengths of Pellon fleece stretched on a wall or otherwise suspended on a vertical surface. The fuzzy surfaces of these fabrics enable you to cut out pieces of the quilt, put them in place, and stand back and analyze them in relation to the whole design.

A reducing glass (just the opposite of a magnifying glass, and available in many quilt shops or office supply stores) or binoculars (use them "backward"). The farther away from a vertical quilt design you can stand, the better you can analyze its progress in terms of color and design. These tools help you do so if you have a small space in which to work.

Camera (with flash capability)—to photograph the quilt in progress, and to use as a tool for analyzing the design. When you look through the viewfinder of the camera, the distractions in the room are eliminated, allowing you to analyze your color choices and your design in general. Snapshots taken of a quilt in progress sometimes lead to other quilt ideas . . . and thus a "working series" evolves.

Good lighting

Time to let the design evolve—Observe your pencil designs and/or quilt pieces on the wall at various times of the day, and from different angles. Sometimes you will come around the corner and upon your design, and see something in it from that angle you never saw in it during hours of working with it at a table.

Remember, good quilts can't be hurried.

Blocks Together

When one combines blocks right out of the patchwork pattern book, placing one block right next to another, the designs that emerge along the edges where the blocks come together are often more interesting than the design within either of the two original blocks. Likewise, when one combines four blocks edge to edge, the design formed where the four blocks meet at the corner becomes the dominant design for the pieced surface. In order to discover these relationships between blocks and thus new designs for quilts, it is necessary to play with the blocks as line designs first.

As you play with the blocks according to the steps below, keep in mind your aim to reach for the unexpected in making combinations of blocks. One way to do this is to put blocks together where one design "reaches into" the neighboring design, camouflaging where one block stops and the next one begins. The goal is to make the viewer of your quilt appreciate the *whole* quilt surface, not look at one block or one pair of blocks and be able to picture what the rest of the quilt looks like.

Steps in Playing with Blocks

1. Go through patchwork pattern books or quilt magazines and choose a number of patchwork patterns that appeal to you. If you are spooked by too many choices, start with four to six patterns; if you want to play with a lot of elements, or you live far away from the photocopy shop, choose a dozen, or more!
2. Draw these patterns to scale on graph paper. Eight-squares-to-the-inch graph paper makes a pattern easy to see. On the graph paper, one tiny square will be equal to 1", life size (Fig. 1).

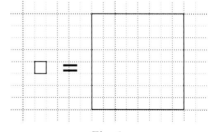

Fig. 1.

Therefore, a book pattern that will be 12" finished will look like this on graph paper:

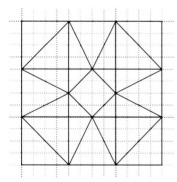

8 squares/inch graph paper

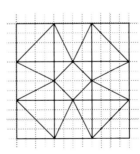

10 squares/inch graph paper

Fig. 2.

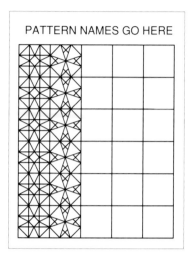

PATTERN NAMES GO HERE

Fig. 3.

Two sizes of graph paper are illustrated on page 11, only to show relative size of the drawings that result. Working with ten-squares-per-inch graph paper means easier multiplication in drafting your designs, but eight-squares-per-inch graph paper is easier on the eyes. *Choose only one scale of graph paper, and use it exclusively* in your drafting and template-making work.

3. Draw a whole column of each design on graph paper (you should be able to draw a column of six blocks on an 8½" x 11" sheet of graph paper), as in Figure 3.

4. Take this paper to a copy center and make at least twenty copies of it, so you have plenty of blocks to work with.

5. *Never cut apart your original graph-paper drawing.* Keep it in your idea book for future photocopying.

6. Cut your photocopies apart, a strip of designs at a time (cut only two sheets of photocopies to start).

Combining Blocks

Take each strip of patterns individually; cut off the three bottom blocks, and place them right next to the three other blocks of the same pattern—do they make an interesting pattern where the six come together?

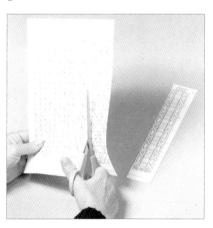 

If so, glue them down onto another sheet of graph paper (the graph-paper lines help you line up your designs easily).

 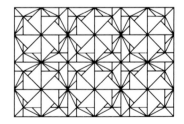

Fig. 4.

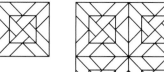
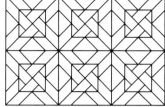

Fig. 5.

Pay particular attention to the motif formed at the corners where four blocks come together: will this motif be more dominant in the overall quilt surface than the main design of the original block?

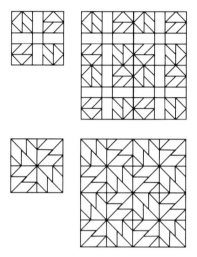

Fig. 6.

This sheet of graph paper with its patterns glued down should be placed in your idea book (see pages 8–9 for a complete description of this special three-ring binder). Keep this exercise and those on tracing paper which follow in a section labeled "Blocks Together" for future reference.

Now take a sheet of tracing paper and place it over each grouping of six blocks in turn. How many different motifs can you find by shading in various areas of this block grouping with a colored pencil?

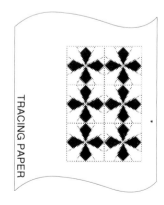

Fig. 7.

For example, a group of six Bachelor's Puzzle blocks could be shaded a number of ways, highlighting various motifs. All of these shadings camouflage where one block stops and the next one begins.

Groupings of Bachelor's Puzzle blocks showing a few of many ways to sprinkle color across the pieced surface to highlight various motifs. Emphasis in many cases is on camouflaging where one block stops and the next one begins.

Playing with Pairs of Patchwork Patterns

1. Take a strip of patterns, and place it next to each of the other strips you have cut apart, to see what designs the combinations form.

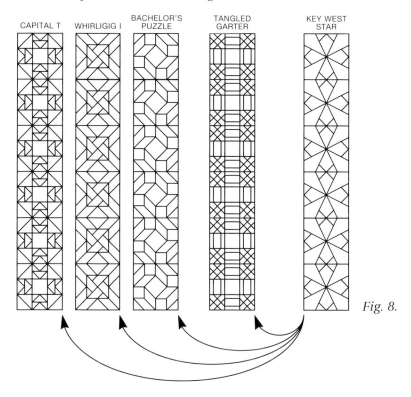

Fig. 8.

2. When you find one that is pleasing—or even slightly interesting—cut off three blocks from each pattern, and glue them down in your idea book side by side.

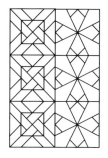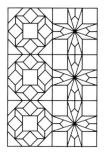

Fig. 9.

3. See what these two patterns look like in groupings of three, thus:

A	B	A
A	B	A
A	B	A

B	A	B
B	A	B
B	A	B

Fig. 10.

In the examples shown below, as well as in selected illustrations that follow in this book, you will note that the line drawings are partly filled in with color. This is done to give you a glimpse of what these block combinations look like when they come alive in real fabric—not to prescribe any specific color scheme for them. As in the color photo on page 14, there are many color possibilities for any grouping of patchwork blocks.

Pairs of patchwork blocks in groupings of three-block columns, with suggestions of color placement

If for some reason you don't find a pleasing combination of blocks the first time around, it's time to go "back to the drawing board" to draw more columns of patchwork patterns onto the graph paper, as shown on page 11.

Checkerboarding Two Patchwork Patterns

Another way to play with two patterns, to see how they combine in the overall quilt surface, is to alternate them checkerboard-style. Using only two patterns, experiment with the following layouts.

1. Cut off four single blocks of one pattern and place them on a piece of graph paper as in Figure 11. Draw a pencil line around the block grouping as shown, so it is obvious that this is a plan for a quilt. Label this "Layout A."

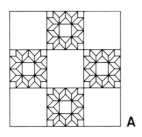

Fig. 11.

2. For the next configuration, cut off five single blocks and place them on a piece of graph paper (all five singles may be of the same pattern, or you may choose an alternate pattern for the center block). Draw a pencil line around the grouping of blocks as in step 1, and label this "Layout B."

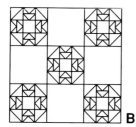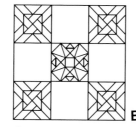

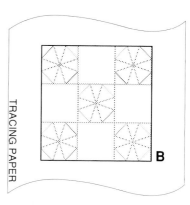

Fig. 12.

Place a piece of tracing paper over each of these layouts (Fig. 13). Trace the square outline around the blocks onto the tracing paper, and write "Layout A" or "Layout B" as appropriate. These groupings of four and five blocks will be used for other exercises, so it is important to make clear which tracing paper drawing goes with which layout.

Fig. 13.

Now find another pattern with which to "fill in the blanks" to create an interesting pieced quilt surface. When you find a combination of blocks that forms an interesting overall surface by camouflaging where one block stops and the next one begins, or one in which the design "reaches into" the neighboring block, glue the companion block down onto the tracing paper (Fig. 14).

Replace tracing paper with a fresh sheet, or slide tracing paper so that the layout below shows through an open working area on the tracing paper.

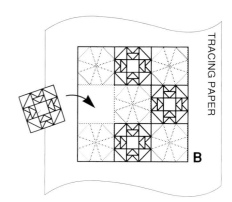

Fig. 14.

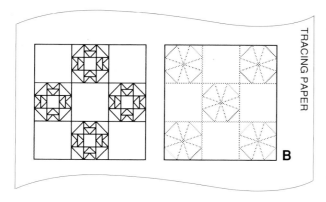

Fig. 15.

Trace outline around layout, label with appropriate layout letter, and then you will be free to search for other smashing "partner blocks" for Layouts A and B, which can be glued down to sheets of tracing paper. *Remember that the blocks glued down on tracing paper can also be used as the basic layouts.*

David's Teenage Quilt by Margaret J. Miller, 1985, San Marcos, California, 72" x 98". David Andrew Miller, son of the author, drew the two pieced blocks (except for the maple leaves in one of them) on graph paper when he was eight or nine years old. He, like other quiltmakers' children, often wanted to color "just like Mommy," and got a chance to use all her newest color pencils by wanting to design a quilt! Collection of David Andrew Miller, Woodinville, Washington.

David's Teenage Quilt (above) is an example of two patchwork patterns checkerboarded in the body of the quilt (with one of those two blocks used alone as the border). This particular combination of blocks can be colored in such a way that one block "reaches" halfway across the neighboring block. In this quilt, the red block reaches into the blue one, camouflaging where one block stops and the other begins.

Playing with More Than Two Patchwork Patterns

Go back to the combinations of patterns you came up with in Playing with Pairs of Patchwork Patterns, page 15.

Now look for a pattern to combine with those pairs to come up with an interesting quilt surface in the configuration shown in Figure 16.

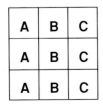

Fig. 16.

In Figure 16, each letter stands for a separate patchwork pattern. An example of actual blocks in this configuration might look like this:

The color photos on this page suggest some of many ways color choice can emphasize camouflaging where one block stops and its neighbor begins.

Now try three patchwork patterns as in Figure 17:

A	B	C	B	A
A	B	C	B	A
A	B	C	B	A

Fig. 17.

Now try these same three patchwork patterns as in Figure 18:

C	B	A	B	C
C	B	A	B	C
C	B	A	B	C

Fig. 18.

(Now you see why you needed so many photocopies!)

Blocks along the Diagonal

One way to extend the checkerboard is to angle the path of blocks diagonally from corner to corner on the quilt. Choose one patchwork pattern, and place five of these on your graph paper in the following configuration:

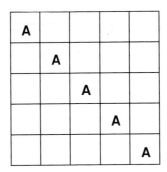 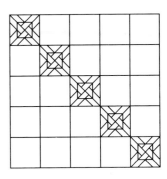

Fig. 19.

Now find two to four different patterns to coordinate with this pattern, to form the following quilt surface:

Five-pattern example

A	B	C	D	E
B	A	B	C	D
C	B	A	B	C
D	C	B	A	B
E	D	C	B	A

Fig. 20.

Four-pattern example

A	B	C	D	D
B	A	B	C	D
C	B	A	B	C
D	C	B	A	B
D	D	C	B	A

Fig. 21.

In the following illustrations, note how varied the pieced surface can be, depending upon the specific blocks chosen.

Five-pattern example

A	E	D	C	B
B	A	E	D	C
C	B	A	E	D
D	C	B	A	E
E	D	C	B	A

Fig. 22.

Three-pattern example

A	B	A	B	C
B	A	B	A	B
C	B	A	B	A
B	C	B	A	B
C	B	C	B	A

Fig. 23.

Once you have glued down your block drawings, rotate the entire paper so that you can look at your design from each of the four sides. Sometimes a more interesting pieced surface emerges when you look at the design upside down or sideways.

A	D	C	B	B
B	A	D	C	D
B	B	A	D	C
C	B	B	A	D
D	C	B	B	A

Fig. 24.

Think about your strategy for the entire quilt surface: will you use a most complex pattern for A, gradually working out to a more open pattern (fewer pieces) for D or E blocks, or will you do the reverse?

Consider the possibility of forming a border around the central quilt surface you create by adding a row of one of the blocks which appears in the interior of the quilt.

To extend this idea one step further, make your basic pattern form an X across the quilt surface.

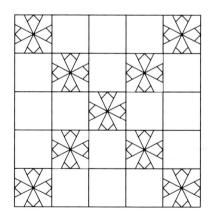
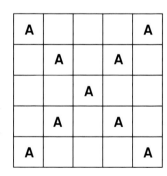

Fig. 25.

There are a number of ways of filling in the blanks around the X block arrangement, two of which appear on page 24.

A	B	C	B	A
B	A	C	A	B
C	C	A	C	C
B	A	C	A	B
A	B	C	B	A

Fig. 26.

A	B	C	B	A
B	A	B	A	B
C	B	A	B	C
B	A	B	A	B
A	B	C	B	A

Fig. 27.

The following charts show various strategies for combining traditional blocks in quilts. Using these models, substitute one patchwork pattern for each letter to try to design an interesting pieced surface.

A	A	A	A	A	A	A
A	C	B	A	B	C	A
A	C	B	A	B	C	A
A	C	B	A	B	C	A
A	C	B	A	B	C	A
A	C	B	A	B	C	A
A	A	A	A	A	A	A

A	A	A	A	A
A	B	C	B	A
A	B	C	B	A
A	B	C	B	A
A	B	C	B	A
A	B	C	B	A
A	A	A	A	A

A	A	A	A	A
A	B	B	B	A
A	B	C	B	A
A	C	C	C	A
A	B	C	B	A
A	B	B	B	A
A	A	A	A	A

B	A	B	A	B	A	B
A	B	A	C	A	B	A
B	A	C	D	C	A	B
A	C	D	D	D	C	A
B	A	C	D	C	A	B
A	B	A	C	A	B	A
B	A	B	A	B	A	B

E	D	A	B	C	C
C	E	D	A	B	C
C	C	E	D	A	B
C	E	D	A	B	C
E	D	A	B	C	C
C	E	D	A	B	C
C	C	E	D	A	B
C	C	C	E	D	A

		B	A	B		
	B	A	E	A	B	
B	A	E	E	E	A	B
A	E	E	F	E	E	A
B	A	E	E	E	A	B
	B	A	E	A	B	
		B	A	B		

A	B	C	D	E
B	C	D	E	A
C	D	E	A	B
D	E	A	B	C
E	A	B	C	D
A	B	C	D	E

Fig. 28.

Stay open to new block arrangements that "happen" as you work with these charts. *Remember,* you are trying to reach for the unexpected through these block combinations, and are keeping the entire quilt surface in mind while playing with blocks, not agonizing about what is going on within any one of them.

Now look over all your block arrangements in these checkerboarding sections. Within each exercise, reverse the positions of the patchwork blocks you have chosen (see Figure 29), to see if a more pleasing arrangement develops.

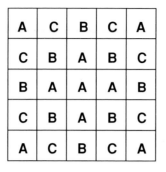

Fig. 29.

Getting Brave: Combining Blocks That Don't Match

You may find that up to this point, you have stayed within one patchwork category to find patterns to combine; you matched Ninepatch patterns with other Ninepatch patterns, Four Patch with Four Patch, and so on. You also probably found it more pleasing to put patterns together where everything matched along the side edges of the blocks, thus:

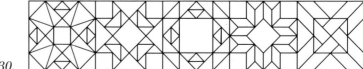

Fig. 30.

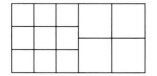

Fig. 31.

Now look for blocks to combine where things don't all match up: this is guaranteed if you match a Ninepatch and a Four Patch, because even the major division lines of the blocks don't meet at the edges (Fig. 31).

Don't be afraid to combine blocks from different patchwork categories; sometimes the areas where things don't meet create interesting backgrounds, or motifs that are more interesting precisely because they don't match.

Block combinations wherein design lines do not match at the edges of the blocks can provide areas of interesting color placement and refreshing ways for blocks to "reach into" neighboring blocks.

The center of Starry, Starry Sampler (below) is an example of "things not matching." The center of this quilt was formed by placing four rectangular blocks in a pinwheel configuration. The light-colored jagged cross in the center of the quilt would not have emerged if the points of the triangles had "matched up" where the edges of the rectangles met.

Starry, Starry Sampler by Margaret J. Miller, 1988, San Marcos, California, 64" x 64". This quilt exhibits many of the design techniques featured in this book, such as distorted blocks, offset design motifs, and nonmatching contiguous blocks. Collection of Jeanne Duncan, Bartlesville, Oklahoma.

Courage!

The Third Dimension in Blocks Together

One way to achieve a more interesting pieced surface when combining traditional patterns is to include at least one block that gives the illusion of a shape behind a shape. This can create the illusion of depth or layers with line design alone—and these effects can be accentuated by color choices later, as the quilt develops.

In the diagram below, the blocks appear to have more than one plane or layer, or lines interrupted by shapes. Both of these design mechanisms give a three-dimensional look to the two-dimensional block.

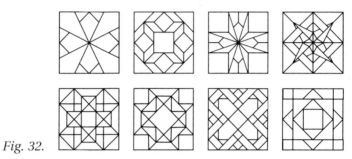

Fig. 32.

The Picture So Far: Some General Principles

As you worked with the blocks in the preceding exercises, some general principles may have become evident. While reading the principles listed below and on page 29, look over the design exercises you have completed so far—do these design principles hold true for the combinations you have chosen?

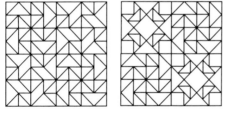

Fig. 33.

a. The more attractive combinations of blocks tend to have one block with many pieces, while its companion has much fewer pieces. If both blocks have approximately the same number of pieces (i.e., the interior of both blocks is divided in a very similar fashion), the result is a mosaic look. But if one block has many pieces and its companion has fewer, the eye has a chance to be led around the quilt surface: it becomes easier to camouflage where one block ends and the next one begins.

b. Some blocks make better alternate blocks than others. Blocks with a strong X feeling to them combine well with many other blocks, because the X shape begins to look like sashing strips between blocks that have been turned on point.

c. Blocks with a central cross (often found in the five-patch category of patchwork patterns) also have a specific effect on block combinations. The north-south and east-west divisions can be made to look like sashing strips between blocks— but they appear and disappear in the quilt surface.

 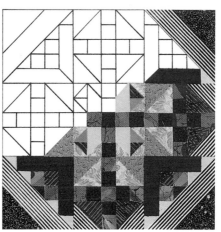

Color placement can accentuate the middle patches of a five-patch block in such a way that they appear to be sashing strips rather than the middle sections of pieced blocks.

Blocks Offset — Yet Still Blocks Together

Go back to cutting single strips of blocks, as on page 12: cut off groupings of three blocks in a column and place next to three like blocks. Next, shift one column of blocks so that the blocks line up not right next to one another, but down or up by an increment.

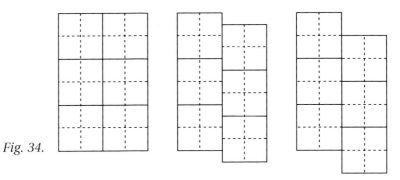

Fig. 34.

This shifting of block position creates new design motifs where the columns of blocks come together. The color photo below illustrates a number of ways to enhance these new block alignments through color placement.

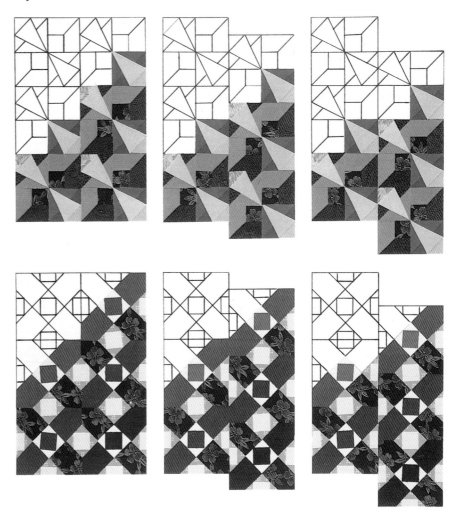

The increment by which the second column of blocks is shifted may be half or one-quarter of a block (common with Four Patch patterns), or by one-third or two-thirds of a block (in the case of Ninepatch patterns).

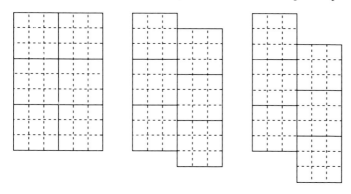

Fig. 35.

In the partially colored Ninepatch blocks below, note the shapes which "twist" around the line where the columns of blocks come together. The direction of twist is reversed in the one-third block offset position from that in the two-thirds block offset.

Watch for the new patterns that develop while this shifting is taking place. When you find an interesting combination, glue it down on graph paper and keep it in the "Blocks Offset" section of your idea book.

Blocks Offset — Two Different Patchwork Patterns

Do the exercise as you did on pages 30–31, but use two different patchwork patterns instead of one.

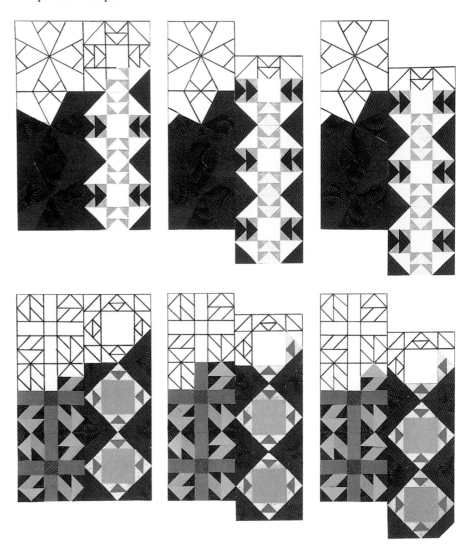

Do not neglect the possibility of gluing another strip of pattern B to the left of pattern A, to get an idea of what the overall surface might look like if these two rows of patterns were alternated, offset, over the whole surface.

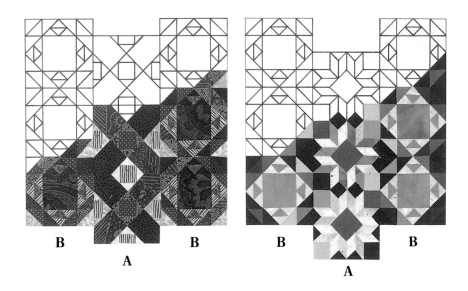

Another design strategy is to place multiple rows of one block in the center. These multiples may be aligned evenly or offset.

More Than Two Patterns—Still Offset

Again working with strips of patterns, each at least three blocks long, try to develop some offset designs using at least three different patchwork patterns.

How to fill in the "odd spaces" at the top and bottom of these designs is covered in the Block and Blank section of this book, pages 39–44.

Offset Patterns—Singles Forming Curves

Fig. 36.

For this exercise, use only one patchwork pattern. Notice that single blocks can be offset in different directions; one need not place all blocks in a downward diagonal only. See if you can find patchwork patterns that make interesting designs when you offset them in the following configurations (one example is done for you; the rest are done in silhouette only):

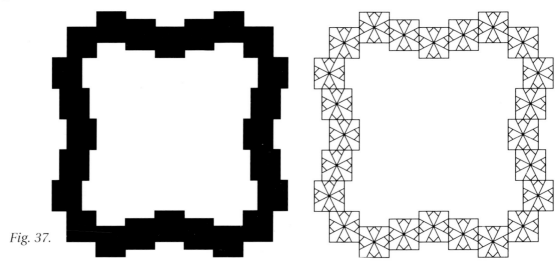

Fig. 37.

The following silhouette block arrangements show how blocks offset can form a border around other blocks set in a conventional manner.

Fig. 38.

Fig. 39.

As you work with these configurations, be sure to note in your idea book any new arrangements you discover. Now, following the models above, use more than one patchwork pattern to establish each configuration.

This method for designing quilt-block layouts can also be used with groups of unrelated blocks, such as friendship blocks and sampler blocks. However, each block must first be bordered with a strip of fabric 1" (or more) wide; this compensates for the fact that the blocks are visually unrelated in design, and allows them to be placed side by side in the quilt surface. To use this planning device for unrelated blocks, the construction paper "blank" you use to represent the block actually represents the block plus its additional border.

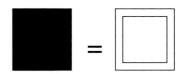

Fig. 40.

This method was used in the planning of the quilt Bernice's Baskets (below). The blocks ranged in size from 6¼" to 7¼" square.

Bernice's Baskets by Margaret J. Miller, 1990, Woodinville, Washington, 83" x 83". The design for this quilt top was begun by offsetting bordered blocks to surround a central area. Note that most blocks when bordered form squares; the central blocks, though square, were bordered unevenly to form rectangles. Blocks by Bernice McCoy Stone and friends. Collection of Bernice McCoy Stone, Kensington, California.

In order to make the group of blocks uniform in size, strips of fabric cut 1¾" wide were sewn to the sides of each block, so that a 9" template could be used to trim each block for final assembly in the quilt. Therefore, the construction-paper blank used to represent the blocks in planning Bernice's Baskets on graph paper measured nine little graph-paper squares to a side.

The following is the plan for this quilt as it appeared in construction-paper blanks. The center of the quilt was later modified, to include rectangular frames around the blocks which were overlapped at the corners (see line drawing of final quilt on page 144).

Fig. 41.

Using a construction-paper blank to represent a block plus its narrow framing border frees the quiltmaker to create circular or otherwise curved paths for the blocks to follow across the quilt surface. A circular arrangement of blocks appears in Figure 39 on page 35.

A serpentine arrangement of blocks was the design jumping-off place for the quilt San Diego Friends II (below). The blocks, all squares, ranged in size from 10" x 10" to 14" x 14". This quilt was designed by cutting construction-paper squares to scale to represent each block; then the squares were moved around a piece of graph paper like puzzle pieces on a puzzle board, until a pleasing arrangement was determined. The flow

San Diego Friends II by Margaret J. Miller, 1990, Woodinville, Washington, 65" x 84". Offset blocks forming a serpentine line across the quilt surface is the design focus of this quilt top. Blocks by friends of Margaret J. Miller, part of a collection of fifty friendship blocks set into a three-quilt series. Collection of the author.

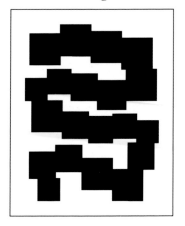

Fig. 42.

of the curve was achieved because some of the blocks are much smaller than others (note that these smallest blocks were used to "turn the corner"). In addition, not all the blocks were offset by the same amount — one block was offset from its neighbor by anywhere from 2" to 8". (See line drawing of this quilt on page 140.)

The same general method was used to design the quilt San Diego Friends III (below).

San Diego Friends III by Margaret J. Miller, 1990, Woodinville, Washington, 71" x 84". Offset blocks forming a spiral is the design focus for this quilt. Blocks by friends of Margaret J. Miller, part of a collection of fifty friendship blocks set into a three-quilt series. Collection of the author.

In this quilt, the blocks were more closely related in size than in San Diego Friends II. The blocks ranged from 12" x 12" to 14" x 14" in size; seventeen were squares and two were rectangles. Note that each block was offset from its neighbor by a much smaller amount (from 2" to 5") than in San Diego Friends II (see line drawing on page 141).

This design could have an even greater dimensional quality to it if much smaller squares were used in the center, graduating in size to the outside end of the spiral. The opposite is also shown below: large blocks in the center, working out to small on the outside edge.

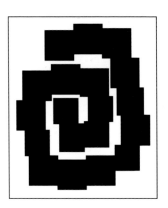

Fig. 43.

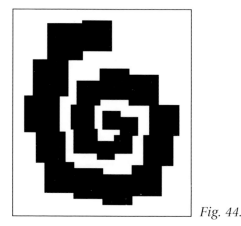

Fig. 44.

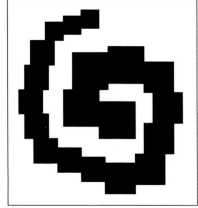

Fig. 45.

Block and Blank Approach to Quilt Design

Up to this point, you have been creating a pieced surface by filling in all the spaces with patterns that came out of a book. In this section, you will be filling only part of the space with a traditional patchwork pattern; the rest is up to you.

Filling in the blanks with original design is not nearly so frightening if first you list what categories of options you have, then select from those categories.

To set up the problem, glue down two block configurations of photocopied patterns, as you did in the Checkerboarding Two Patchwork Patterns section, steps 1 and 2, pages 16–17. (Or, use some of the configurations you have already glued down, either on graph paper or on tracing paper.)

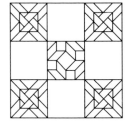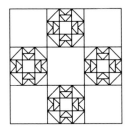

Fig. 46.

Problem: A blank space to fill.

Options for filling that space:

1) straight lines (horizontals and verticals)
2) diagonal lines (two directions)
3) curved lines (beyond the scope of this book)

Let's consider these options one at a time.

Horizontals Only

Single horizontal line dividing the space evenly

Single horizontal line dividing the space unevenly

Multiple horizontal lines dividing the space evenly

Multiple horizontal lines dividing the space unevenly

Verticals Only

Single vertical line dividing the space evenly

Single vertical line dividing the space unevenly

Multiple vertical lines dividing the space evenly

Multiple vertical lines dividing the space unevenly

Horizontals and Verticals Together

Single horizontal and single vertical, dividing the space evenly

Single horizontal and single vertical, dividing the space unevenly

Multiple horizontals and multiple verticals, dividing the space evenly

Multiple horizontals and multiple verticals, dividing the space unevenly

Diagonals, Left to Right

Single diagonal, dividing the space evenly

Single diagonal, dividing the space unevenly

Multiple diagonals, dividing the space evenly

Multiple diagonals, dividing the space unevenly

Diagonals, Right to Left

Single diagonal, dividing the space evenly

Single diagonal, dividing the space unevenly

Multiple diagonals, dividing the space evenly

Multiple diagonals, dividing the space unevenly

Diagonals in Both Directions

Single diagonal each direction, dividing the space evenly

Single diagonal each direction, dividing the space unevenly

Multiple diagonals both directions, dividing the space evenly

Multiple diagonals both directions, dividing the space unevenly

Combinations of the above options are endless.

HOW TO CHOOSE AN OPTION. To do the design exercises in this section, label each of the block configurations you have glued down with a letter ("Layout A" and "Layout B").

A B *Fig. 47.*

Place a sheet of tracing paper over the layouts; the actual pencil lines of the exercises will be placed on the tracing paper only. (Don't forget to label the tracing paper also as "Layout A" or "Layout B," so that later you can get back to your good ideas.)

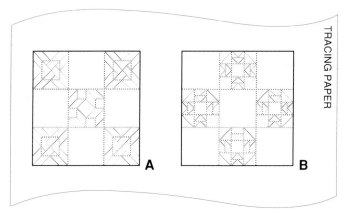

Fig. 48.

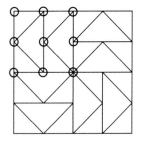

Fig. 49. Dutchman's Puzzle pattern: a Four Patch pattern; design points are circled in upper left-hand patch of block.

Look for the design points and design lines you have as givens within the blocks. A **design line** is any line drawn within the perimeter of the block. When a block is constructed of fabric, the design lines are the seams that hold the fabric pieces of the block together. A **design point** is any position (spot) in the block where two design lines intersect, including the corners of the block. Design points also occur where interior design lines intersect with the perimeter of the block (Fig. 49).

Remember: you are trying to make a pleasing pieced surface design, to *reach for the unexpected* in that design, and to *camouflage* where one block stops and the other begins so that the viewer cannot look at one block in your quilt and envision what the rest of the quilt looks like.

For example, let's say you have the following blocks and you are trying to "fill in the blanks" to create a quilt surface. The obvious design points to connect are the following:

Fig. 50.

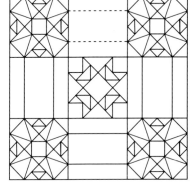

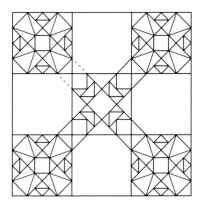

But wouldn't it be visually more interesting—more unexpected—to connect the design points as in Figure 51.

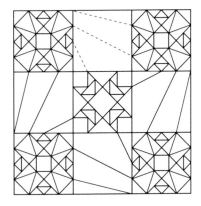

Fig. 51.

Another option you have for filling in the blanks is to extend design lines which are already present in the blocks.

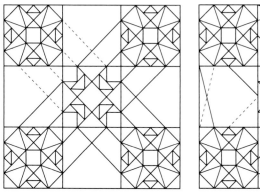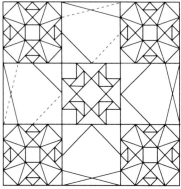

Fig. 52.

Look for chances to create the illusion that one shape is overlapping another one. For instance, say that in your blank you have drawn the following lines, and you want to connect the indicated design points:

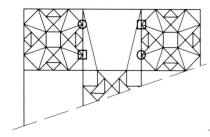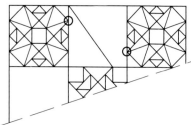

Fig. 53.

Try interrupting the lines between design points with the shape you've already outlined in the blank space. This creates the illusion that one shape is behind another one.

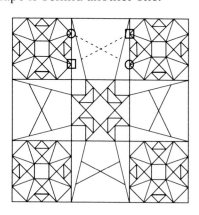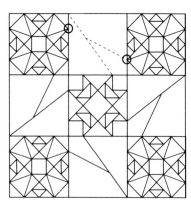

Fig. 54.

To extend this idea, you may choose to "reach into" a neighboring block to find a design point to connect with a design point at the edge of the block. But the line connecting these two design points may be interrupted by a shape in one or both blocks.

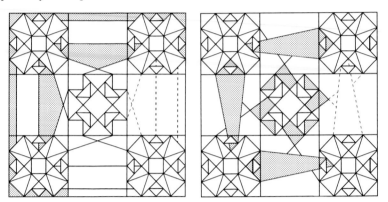

Fig. 55.

Another option you have is to connect design points with other than a straight line: consider using a bent line to connect any two design points, or to extend a design line.

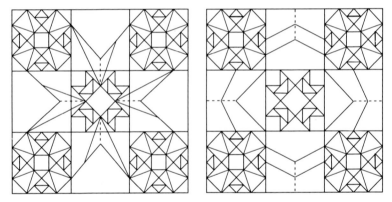

Fig. 56.

The dotted lines in the drawings above are seams necessary for the construction of the block. Any time a "point" comes out into an open area of a block, it is necessary to draw a seam from that point to the edge of the block for construction purposes. Without such a seam, a "bubble" would form around the point in the open area.

The block and blank approach to quilt design is a useful tool for filling open spaces such as those created by overlapping blocks (pages 51–57) and offset blocks (pages 30–39), and for designing innovative spaces between blocks as well as around them in borders (pages 65–118).

Maneuvers in the Interior

Up to this point we have been considering the possibilities for creating patterns by taking traditional blocks right out of pattern books and placing them one right next to the other, offsetting them, or alternating them with a block of our own design.

In this section we will investigate the possibilities for altering the interior spaces of the block, to create multiple patterns from one traditional quilt block. We will do this by maneuvering design lines (which are ultimately seams in a finished quilt block) and design points (places in the block where two or more design lines intersect).

Let us consider the Four Patch design Dutchman's Puzzle as an example. This is a simple design in which each of the four patches is identical, consisting of two equal triangles, each filling half the patch. The movement within the block comes from the direction of the triangles in the patches: all the triangles point toward the outside edges of the block.

Design Points and Design Lines within the Block

Before you begin to maneuver design points and design lines in any block, first draw the block in a traditional manner, just as it appears in the pattern book (Fig. 57).

Next, identify the major design points and design lines. In Dutchman's Puzzle, these would be:

1. the apex of each triangle and
2. the dividing line between the triangles within each patch (Fig. 58).

The line dividing the patches we will call the "midline."

For ease of discussion, let us consider that each patch measures four units on a side. For your first maneuver, move the apex of the triangle one unit toward the midline of the block. (For each maneuver, redraw the Dutchman's Puzzle block. Consider your starting point to be the traditional drafting of Dutchman's Puzzle, not the previous maneuver.)

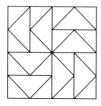

Fig. 57.

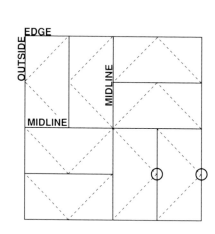

Fig. 58.

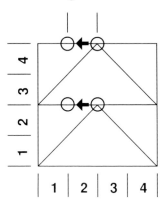

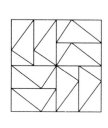

Fig. 59.

Next, move the apex of the triangle one unit toward the outside edge of the block (Fig. 60). (Remember to keep the triangles pointing the proper direction; all should point outward. On the other hand, *from drafting mistakes great quilts are born* — so don't disregard a design with a mistake.)

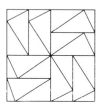

Fig. 60.

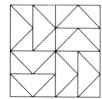 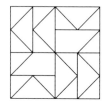 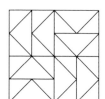

Fig. 61.

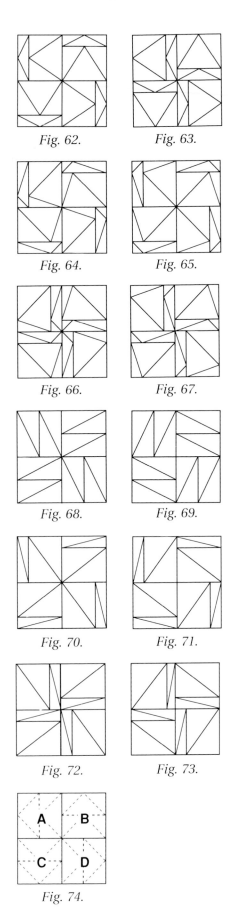

Fig. 62.   *Fig. 63.*

Fig. 64.   *Fig. 65.*

Fig. 66.   *Fig. 67.*

Fig. 68.   *Fig. 69.*

Fig. 70.   *Fig. 71.*

Fig. 72.   *Fig. 73.*

Fig. 74.

Now, move the dividing line between the triangles up one unit toward the outside edge of the block (see upper right-hand patch in Figure 62), keeping the apex of the triangle in its original (center) position.

Next, move the dividing line between triangles down one unit toward the midline of the block, keeping the apex of the triangle in its center position (Fig. 63).

Next, perform two maneuvers at once:

1. move dividing line up one unit (toward outside edge of block)
2. move apex of triangle toward midline one unit (Fig. 64).

Another double maneuver: dividing line moves up one unit, apex of triangle moves toward outside edge one unit (Fig. 65).

Move dividing line down (toward midline) one unit, and apex of triangle toward midline one unit (Fig. 66).

Move dividing line down (toward midline) one unit, and apex of triangle toward outside one unit (Fig. 67).

The next series of maneuvers is going to make it appear that one design line has been eliminated.

Leave dividing line between triangles in middle, move apex of triangle all the way to the outside edge of the block (Fig. 68).

Leave dividing line in middle, move apex of triangle all the way to the midline of the block (Fig. 69).

Move dividing line up one unit, apex of triangle all the way to the edge of the block (Fig. 70).

Move dividing line up one unit, apex of triangle all the way to midline of the block (Fig. 71).

Move dividing line down one unit, apex of triangle all the way to edge of the block (Fig. 72).

Move dividing line down one unit, apex of triangle all the way to midline of the block (Fig. 73).

Now, assign a letter to each of the four patches of Dutchman's Puzzle, such as A, B, C, D (Fig. 74).

Further variations of Dutchman's Puzzle can be achieved by performing one maneuver in patches A and D, another maneuver in patches B and C.

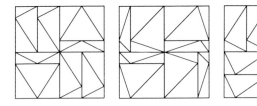

Fig. 75.

Or, perform one maneuver in A and C, another maneuver in B and D.

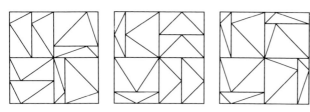

Fig. 76.

A more radical move is to take the design point at the midline end only of the line which divides the two triangles, and move it toward the center; then move this one design point toward the outside edge of the block, as seen below.

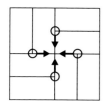 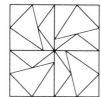 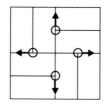 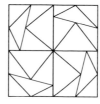

Fig. 77.

Perform the same two maneuvers with the design point at the outside-edge end only of the line that divides the two triangles, thus:

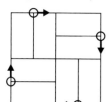 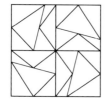 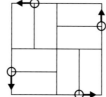 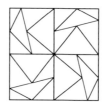

Fig. 78.

As you perform the various maneuvers, notice that the pinwheel blades in the center of the block change shape from wider to narrower. You may plan a quilt which consists of a number of the maneuvered variations of Dutchman's Puzzle, wherein the broader pinwheels will be in the center of the quilt, and the narrower ones will form the border. Or, you may plan the opposite—the narrowest pinwheels will be in the center (where they appear almost starlike), and the broader ones will form the border.

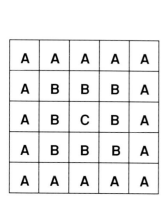 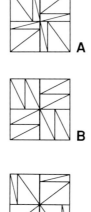 

Fig. 79.

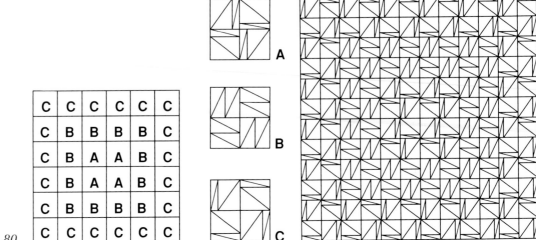

C	C	C	C	C	C
C	B	B	B	B	C
C	B	A	A	B	C
C	B	A	A	B	C
C	B	B	B	B	C
C	C	C	C	C	C

Fig. 80.

What variations can you achieve by maneuvering design points and design lines from the following blocks?

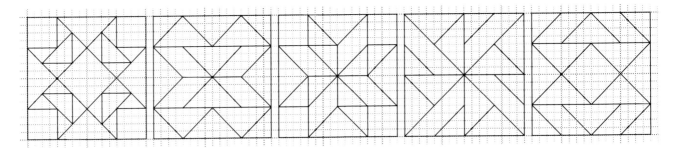

Fig. 81.

Invisible Design Points

Not all the design points to be moved around need be visible in the block; for example, in St. Louis Star, the design points maneuvered in the following variations are the points of the diamond that appear to be behind the rays emanating from the center.

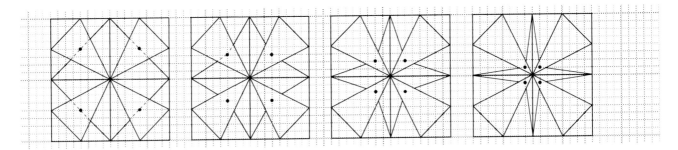

Fig. 82.

Major Division Lines (Asymmetrical Blocks)

A whole new world of design is opened up when one starts to maneuver not merely design points and/or design lines, but the major division lines within the block which determine its category of patchwork.

For example, the lines within the blocks below are those that determine in which category a given pattern falls: four patch, ninepatch, or five patch.

Four Patch **Ninepatch** **Five Patch**

Fig. 83.

These division lines may be interrupted by a shape in the block, and may not be continuous from one edge of the block to the other, as in the examples below:

Ninepatch   **Four Patch**   **Five Patch**

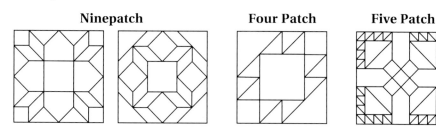

Fig. 84.

Major division lines normally divide the interior of the block evenly; the maneuver we are going to apply will create uneven divisions of that interior space. In Figure 85 (left) is the normal procedure for drafting a Ninepatch block into a 12" square; the divisions within the block are equal and measure 4" on a side. At right is a distorted version of that 12" block; the major division lines are placed 2", 4", and 6" from the edges of the block.

To draft a traditional block into these two grids, first draft the block in the traditional (evenly divided) grid. Then in the distorted grid, proceed one patch at a time, drafting the individual patches of the traditional block in the patches of the distorted version. The pattern Card Trick in its traditional and its distorted versions would look like those in Figure 86.

Not all designs can be distorted by merely connecting obvious design points. In the block Keywest Beauty, for example, merely connecting design points at the edges of the block would yield the results shown in Figure 87.

To make this a meaningful pattern, we must notice that the important aspect of the diagonal lines AB, CD, EF, and GH is not that they *cross* at the center of the block, but that they *meet* at that point. In the distorted grid, they must be drawn not as continuous lines AB, CD, etc., but as segments of lines: from A to the center of the middle patch, B to the center, and so on.

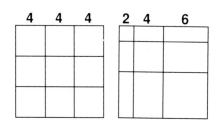

Fig. 85.

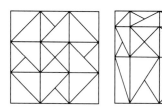

Fig. 86.

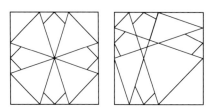

Fig. 87.

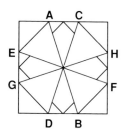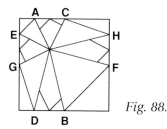

Fig. 88.

In the diagrams of other selected blocks and their distorted versions below, notice that the reason the distorted versions are so dramatic is that new angles are introduced into the traditional pieced design. The majority of angles found in four-, five-, and ninepatch categories are 45° and 90°; when you introduce other size angles into the block, you breathe new design life into it.

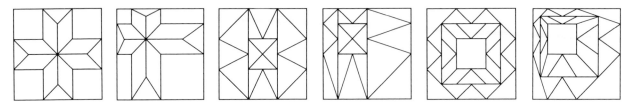

Fig. 89.

Consider other distortions of the basic block: perhaps you will distort the major division lines in one direction only.

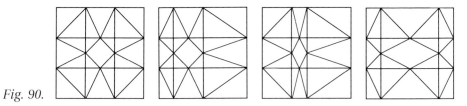

Fig. 90.

The distortion need not be a "narrow-wider-widest" distortion; other combinations could be considered and applied in one or both directions.

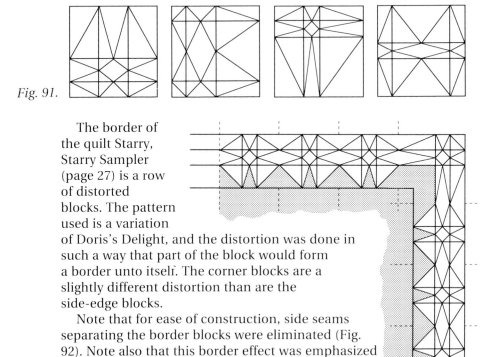

Fig. 91.

The border of the quilt Starry, Starry Sampler (page 27) is a row of distorted blocks. The pattern used is a variation of Doris's Delight, and the distortion was done in such a way that part of the block would form a border unto itself. The corner blocks are a slightly different distortion than are the side-edge blocks.

Note that for ease of construction, side seams separating the border blocks were eliminated (Fig. 92). Note also that this border effect was emphasized by using the blue fabric from the center of the quilt for part of the block. This was purposely done to camouflage where the quilt stopped and the border began.

Fig. 92.

The Perimeter of the Block

Perhaps the most dramatic maneuvering technique is that of changing the position of the four design lines that define the block: its outside edges.

When our goal is to reach for the unexpected in pieced surface design, one sure way to do so is to *change the angles* we are accustomed to seeing in patchwork blocks. When you draft a square traditional patchwork block into a rectangular space, you are forced to change the angles within the block. The horizontal and vertical lines do not change, but every diagonal line does change angle; this then opens up a whole new world of quilt design.

Before maneuvering the outer design lines (the block edges), draft the traditional block as a square (Fig. 93).

Then, draw a rectangle. The space inside the rectangle is divided in the same proportion as that inside the square (traditional) block; if it is a Ninepatch block, your first step is to divide the space in thirds both horizontally and vertically (Fig. 94).

Complete the drafting of the block into these newly shaped patches.

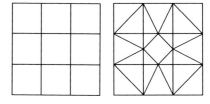

Fig. 93.

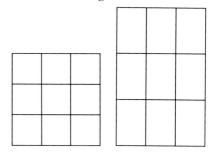

Fig. 94.

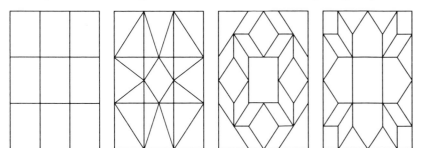

Fig. 95.

Overlapping Blocks for New Layouts

Another way to consider traditional pieced blocks is to overlap parts of them to create "chains of design" that undulate across the pieced surface. Since this often involves assembling blocks of two different sizes and shapes in the same pieced surface, the quilter needs to understand the block and blank approach to quilt design (pages 39–44) and to be at ease with unconventional piecing techniques before attempting to assemble such a quilt.

Single Patterns Overlapped

Choose a number of blocks which have "empty corners," such as those diagrammed below.

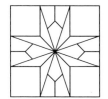 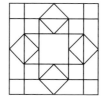

Fig. 96.

Draw a number of these patterns to scale on graph paper, and make at least a dozen photocopies of your sheet of graph-paper drawings, as in Steps in Playing with Blocks, page 11.

Cut out nine single blocks of one pattern.

First, glue four blocks down, one next to another, on graph paper to form a larger square.

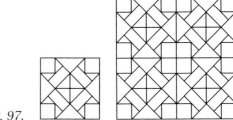

Fig. 97.

Next, take the other five photocopied blocks and glue them down onto another sheet of graph paper in the configuration shown in Figure 98, overlapping the corner patches of each block.

This, then, is the jumping-off place for pieced surface design. To complete this overlapped design, place tracing paper over your glued arrangement, and using the block and blank approach to quilt design, begin to add design lines, connecting design points and extending design lines to make a cohesive pieced surface of this grouping of blocks (Fig. 99).

Continue to explore this overlapping design strategy by combining blocks together (Fig. 97) and blocks overlapped (Fig. 98) in the same design. Figure 100 shows just one of many possible resulting pieced surfaces.

Fig. 98.

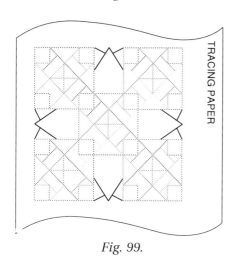

Fig. 99.

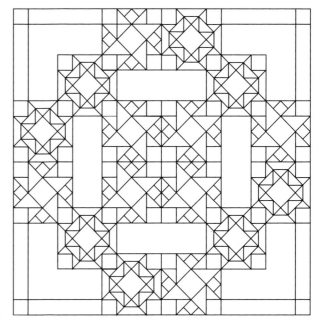

Fig. 100.

Multiple Patterns Overlapped

The next challenge is to incorporate several patterns into the same overlapped surface; it is not necessary to choose only patterns that have an "empty patch" in the corners. One might choose patterns on the basis of complexity, placing the most complex patterns in the center of the quilt, working out to more open (less complex) patterns at the border, as shown below.

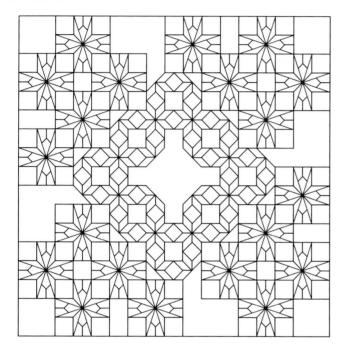

Fig. 101.

Or, the opposite approach may be in order, placing the most complex patterns around the edge of the quilt, forming a dense border, and using the most open blocks in the center of the quilt surface, as in the example below.

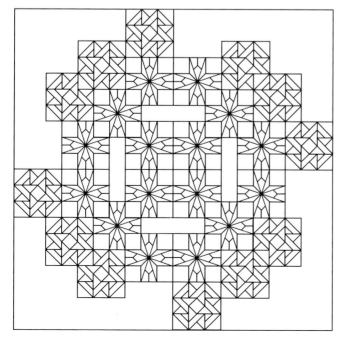

Fig. 102.

Overlapping Other-Than-Open Corners

The principle of overlapping patchwork patterns can also be used in overlapping the points of diamonds and the sides of square blocks. This approach is for the quiltmaker who is at ease with the block and blank approach to quilt design (pages 39–44), and who is ready for some advanced piecing techniques.

For this discussion, we will consider 12" blocks, either Four Patch or Ninepatch patterns. We will consider overlapping a block "on point" (also called a diamond-shaped block) over two strips of square blocks on either side of it. Blocks that have diagonal lines in either corner or edge patches are especially appropriate for this overlapping technique. The corners of the diamond can then overlap either the edge of the block, or the seam where two blocks come together.

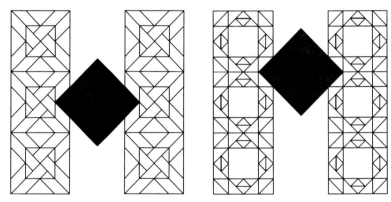

Fig. 103.

Though one may use photocopies of patterns to establish the basic combination of blocks and their path around the quilt, it is best to draft the entire quilt surface to scale on graph paper before making templates and cutting fabric, since photocopying any drawing distorts its size and shape somewhat. This distortion is why you can photocopy a drawing of a block, cut out the photocopy, and not be able to align the photocopied block with the block drawn on the original graph paper.

Note that a block on the diagonal ("on point") will not necessarily come up to the lines you may want it to on graph paper: a 12" block on point may have to be drafted slightly larger or smaller to accommodate a given pieced surface. You must give yourself permission to make slight adjustments in the final templates to make a cohesive pieced surface. This is a good place to use the block and blank approach to quilt design.

To begin, play with photocopied strips of square blocks and singles of them turned on point, trying to find interesting block combinations in the formats shown in Figure 103. Glue down one strip of at least six square blocks on a piece of graph paper.

To determine the width of the space into which the diamond block will be drafted, keep in mind that a diamond shape occupies 1.41 times the linear space that the same shape occupies when positioned as a square. In other words, a 12" block would occupy 12" on a given line; a 12" block on point, or used as a diamond shape, would occupy 1.41 x 12", or 16.92" (Fig. 104).

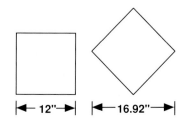

Fig. 104.

It is not practical to work with 16.92 as a unit of measurement in patchwork. Therefore, round this figure up to the next logical number easily divided by three (for Ninepatch blocks) or by two (for Four Patch blocks), which would be 18. The general rule of thumb is that a diamond shape occupies 1.5 times the space the same-size square occupies (Fig. 105).

Next, notice how far the diamond invades the square blocks. Using the pattern Flower Pot as an example, we see that the diamond could invade the strip of straight blocks 6", if it were to extend all the way to the midpoint of the block. Another option is to invade only 3", or one-quarter of the way across the block.

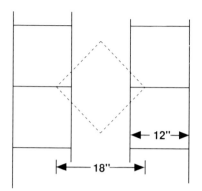

Fig. 105.

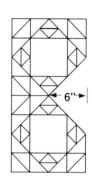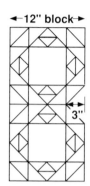

Fig. 106.

If the diamond-shaped block is going to overlap the straight blocks by 6" on either side, and the 12" block used as a diamond shape occupies 18", then 18 − 2(6") = 6" or the width of the space between the strips of straight blocks (Fig. 107). If the diamond-shaped block is going to overlap the straight blocks by 3" on either side, then 18" − 2(3") = 12". The strips of straight blocks in this case would be separated by a space 12" wide.

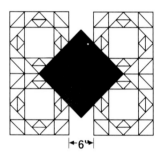

Fig. 107.

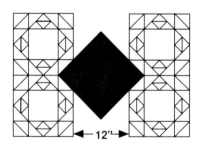

Fig. 108.

The general formula is: corner-to-corner measurement of diamond-shaped block minus the number of inches it invades the straight blocks on both sides equals the width of space between rows of straight blocks.

Using this formula, glue down a second strip of straight blocks to the right of the first strip you glued down, at the proper distance away from them.

Glue one of the diamond-shaped blocks in place between the two straight strips. You may notice that the fit of this block into the space is not exact, as previously discussed.

Using liquid correction fluid or blank paper cut to shape, eliminate all design lines in the areas where the diamond-shaped blocks will invade the straight strips (Fig. 109).

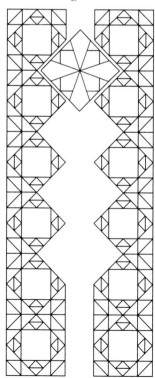

Fig. 109.

In the next two available spaces, pencil in the edges of the next diamond-shaped blocks (Fig. 110).

Now draft the diamond-shaped blocks in place (Fig. 111).

As long as you are redrafting the pattern, consider maneuvering design points of the diamond-shaped blocks, as on pages 44–47. In the example below, the only design points moved were the free corners of the diamond-shaped block. The range of design possibilities goes from overlapping the diamond-shaped blocks, as in Figure 111, to separating them completely, as in Figure 112.

To develop this drawing into a quilt plan, place tracing paper over the drawing, and using the block and blank approach to quilt design, add design lines that relate the open points of the diamond blocks to the rows of square blocks (Fig. 113).

Fig. 110.

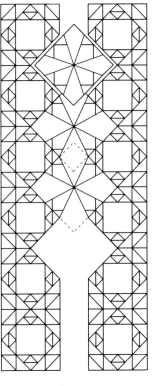

Fig. 111.

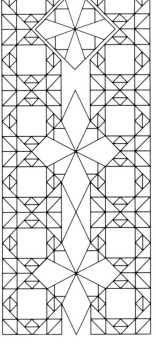

Fig. 112.

Fig. 113.

The next avenue of exploration involves choosing diamond-shaped blocks that are much larger or much smaller than the straight blocks for overlapping.

Fig. 114.

When you are overlapping diamonds and squares, be sure to consider all your alternatives: in Figure 115, the diamonds on the left are under the squares; the diamonds on the right are over the squares.

Blocks used

Fig. 115.

A similar variation was used in Figure 116. However, in the center of this example, the diamonds' points are over the square; on the outer edges, they are under the corner squares.

Blocks used

Fig. 116.

Superimposing One Block over Another

If we carry the idea of overlapping blocks one step further, we can create the illusion that 1) the design from one block or sashing strip can be seen "through" another block, or 2) that a block has been laid on top of a block below it.

An example of the first possibility is the position of the frog blocks in Allen's Teenage Quilt (below).

Allen's Teenage Quilt by Margaret J. Miller, 1988, San Marcos, California, 54" x 93". Examples of superimposing one block over another appear in the star blocks in the center. The frog blocks at the corners of the central oval have been "pushed" into the checkerboard sashing strip. Collection of Allen Edward Miller, son of the author, Woodinville, Washington.

The frog blocks are at the four corners of the central medallion in this quilt. The predictable way of using them would have been to place them at the precise corners of the rectangular center of the quilt, and have them surrounded by the checkerboard sashing strips that separate the center of the quilt from the row of border blocks (Fig. 117). But in an effort to reach for the unexpected, the sashing strips were brought into the frog block on two sides, thus camouflaging where the block stops and the sashing strip begins (Fig. 118).

The same kind of camouflage was used in the border of Springtime Memories II (below).

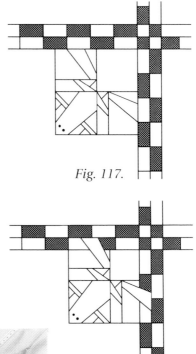

Fig. 117.

Fig. 118.

Springtime Memories II by Margaret J. Miller, 1990, Woodinville, Washington, 68" x 68". Dominant design characteristics include blocks bordered and offset to form a circle around central block; flying geese border features multiple fabrics which camouflage where the quilt's center stops and the border begins. Blocks by customers of The Quilt Barn, Puyallup, Washington, as part of the "Springtime Memories" quilt block contest, spring 1990. Quilt top temporarily in collection of Evelyn M. Griffin, Puyallup, Washington.

In the area where the flying geese triangles meet the blocks, the predictable choice would have been a single fabric filling the triangular shapes between the "wings" of the geese. But by using two fabrics to fill those triangular shapes, a more three-dimensional feeling is created than if only one fabric were used.

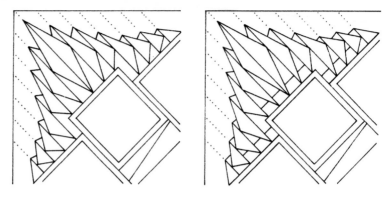

Fig. 119.

Cody Mazuran, in her quilt Gathering Basket: A Signature Quilt (below), has achieved an almost dreamlike quality in the way she has overlapped the corners of her diamond blocks.

Gathering Basket: A Signature Quilt by Cody M. Mazuran, 1989, Salt Lake City, Utah, 53" x 54". Multitudes of embroidered signature strips made this an especially challenging project. The overlapping of the outer diamonds and the central one is especially gracefully done; note that the corner blocks seem to zoom out of the center of the quilt because of the "pedestals" formed by groupings of the signature strips. Signature strips by friends of the quiltmaker; blocks made, assembled, and quilted by Cody M. Mazuran. Collection of the quiltmaker.

The elements she had to combine in this quilt were small 6½" and 7" blocks, and numerous 1½" wide strips with signatures embroidered on them. All the blocks have a double border: one part is a colored fabric that enhances the block within, the other a combination of signature strips punctuated with colored squares at the corners.

Two predictable ways of connecting the outer diamond blocks to the center one might have been the following:

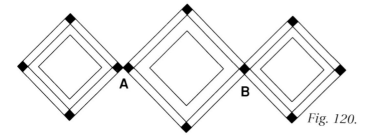

Fig. 120.

But by overlapping the corners of the diamond blocks and the border of the central block on its outer signature strip border, Cody achieved a special cohesiveness in this challenging group of elements.

Fig. 121.

Notice also how the north, south, east, and west diamonds overlap the signature strips that form an inner border around the quilt.

An opaque, layered effect achieved by superimposing one block over another is evident at the corners of the inner border on the Friendship Quilters Guild Banner (below).

Friendship Quilters Guild Banner by Margaret J. Miller, 1984, San Marcos, California, 49" x 55". Multiple shape blocks gathered in the center distinguish this quilt, as do the overlapping motifs in the inner border. Blocks made by early members of Friendship Quilters Guild of Poway, California, formed in 1980. Quilted by guild members and now owned by Friendship Quilters Guild, Poway, California.

Two predictable ways of designing this border might be the following:

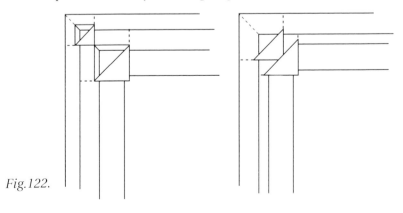

Fig. 122.

But in order to reach for the unexpected, the corner square was enlarged, and a smaller square superimposed on it, to give a more three-dimensional look to the flat quilt surface. The dotted lines in Figure 123 are seam lines that are necessary to assemble this pieced design.

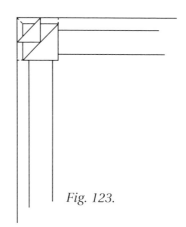

Fig. 123.

Ogee Patterns

Up to this point, we have considered patchwork patterns as squares. For this section, we will be turning the squares on point and considering them as diamond shapes.

In the world of standard repeat patterns, there is a special category of diamond repeat patterns called ogee patterns. In this repeat, the side edges of the diamonds have been transformed into curves; but for our purposes, the same shape can be achieved by cutting off two corners of certain patchwork blocks, and turning them on point (Fig. 125). To prepare for this section, take your strips of photocopied patchwork patterns, cut the blocks apart, and turn them on point. Select patterns that make a pleasing design when two of the corners are trimmed away.

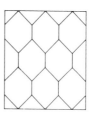

Fig. 124.

Fig. 125.

You will be doing the same design exercises we did in the first section of this chapter (pages 11–29); but in this case, it is important to look at the layouts (ogee grids) you devise from two sides. Since the ogee pattern is not symmetrical, it will form very different designs, depending on the edge from which it is viewed.

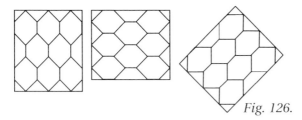

Fig. 126.

In the following exercises, "pattern" or "block" refers to a block which has been transformed so it can fit the ogee grid (the block is turned on point, with two corners cut away).

First, choose one pattern and fill every ogee grid cell with it (Fig. 127).

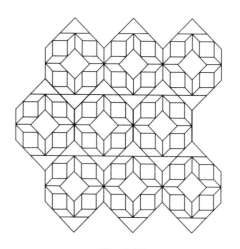

Fig. 127.

Next, find two patterns and arrange them checkerboard style in the ogee grid.

Fig. 128.

See what these same two patterns look like in rows, arranged either horizontally or vertically.

Fig. 129.

Fig. 130.

Now, try to find multiple patterns to combine in the ogee grid; in the charts below, each letter stands for a different patchwork pattern within any one design.

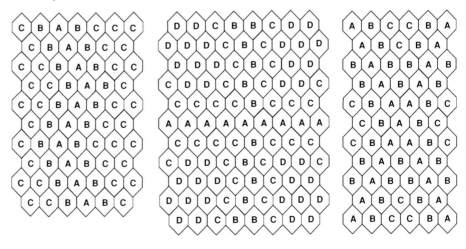

Pathways among the Blocks

The traditional method of assembling a grouping of quilt blocks into a quilt surface involves separating each pair of blocks by a strip of fabric called a sashing strip. Normally the piecing proceeds by alternating a block and a sashing strip until a row of blocks is completed. Once the rows are all sewn together, each row is sewn to a sashing strip that is as long as the quilt is wide (Fig. 131). These rows of blocks and sashing strip units are then sewn together until the entire quilt top is complete.

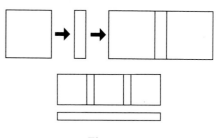

Fig. 131.

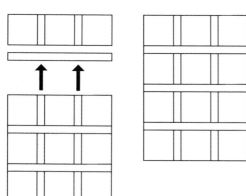

Fig. 132.

Sometimes where the sashing strips come together at the corner of a block, a square of fabric, known as a setting square, is added for interest.

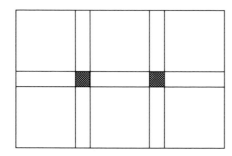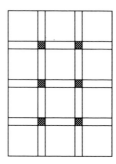

Fig. 133.

In order to reach for the unexpected in pieced surface design, it is helpful to think of the area between and around the blocks as a meaningful setting for the blocks, rather than a rigid separation of one block from another. This goes with the idea that we are aiming for a pieced surface wherein the viewer cannot look at just one block and predict what the balance of the quilt looks like.

In that spirit, then, the following exercises are intended to force you,

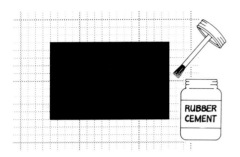

Fig. 134.

Fig. 135.

in methodical, measured steps, to get away from separating blocks with only plain strips of fabric.

To prepare for these design exercises, adhere a piece of graph paper to a piece of colored construction paper with rubber cement. Prepare at least two graph-paper/construction-paper sets in this fashion (Fig. 134). Using the graph-paper lines as cutting guides, cut out as many 1½" squares as you can. Each of these colored squares represents one quilt block—either pieced or appliquéd. By using colored squares of paper to represent quilt blocks, you will not be distracted by the specific content of each block, but rather will be able to focus on the environment you want to create for those blocks.

Varying the Width of Sashing Strips

Take two large (11" x 17") sheets of graph paper. On one, glue four construction-paper squares (colored side up) in the center of the paper, separated to the width of one small square on the graph paper (Fig. 135). Surround this grouping of four by another ring of blocks—but this time, make the sashing strips *two* small squares wide. Notice that the sashing strip that separates the center blocks will always remain one square wide to the edges of the layout.

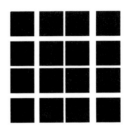

Fig. 136.

Surround this grouping of blocks by another ring of blocks—but make the sashing strips *three* small squares wide—and continue in this fashion until you have three complete rings around the original grouping of four blocks. The sashing strips separating your last ring of blocks from the previous one should be four small squares wide.

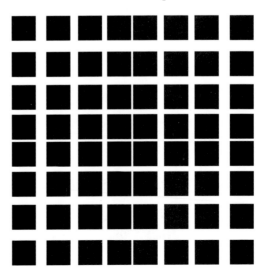

Fig. 137.

This is the strategy used in planning Inner City Star (below).

The sashing strips are ½" wide (finished) in the center of the quilt, and increase in width by ½" as they approach the edges of the quilt. Notice how this seems to intensify the design in the center of the piece.

On your second piece of graph paper, glue four construction-paper squares in the center of the paper, this time separated by *four* small squares of the graph paper.

Inner City Star by Margaret J. Miller, 1982, San Marcos, California, 69" x 69". The varied-width sashing strips focus attention on the central area of the quilt, where the sashing strips are narrowest. Collection of the author.

Fig. 138.

Continue gluing down rings of blocks around this center grouping of four blocks as in Figures 135–137, except this time, decrease the width of the sashing strips separating each ring of blocks from the preceding ring by one small square.

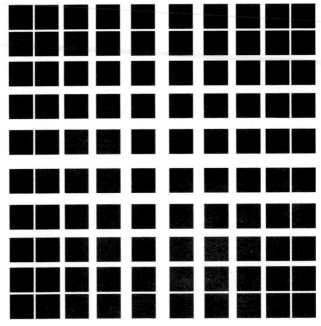

Fig. 139.

Another application of varying the width of sashing strips is exemplified by the quilt Hearthfires Endure (below).

Hearthfires Endure by Margaret J. Miller, 1985, San Marcos, California, 59" x 59". Note that the sashing strips separating rows of simple strip-pieced blocks are placed in one direction only, and that they narrow as they approach the upper left-hand corner of the quilt. Part of the eight-quilt "Strips That Sizzle" series. Collection of the author.

In this piece, the sashing strips are wider in the lower right corner of the quilt, and become gradually narrower as they approach the upper left corner. There are no sashing strips in the opposite direction.

Variations on this theme are illustrated in Figure 140.

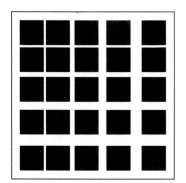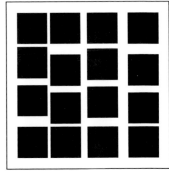

Fig. 140.

Varying the Content of Sashing Strips

On another piece of graph paper (eight squares to the inch), glue twelve of these construction-paper blanks—colored side up—so that they form a quilt top with blocks as in Figure 141. The grouping has four rows of three blocks each, and each block is separated by two small blocks (¼") on the graph paper. Label this "Block Grouping A."

On a second piece of graph paper (also eight squares to the inch), glue twelve more construction-paper blanks colored side up so that they are more widely spaced, creating wider pathways among the blocks in which to design a more meaningful environment for them (Fig. 142). In this layout there are four rows of three blocks each, each block separated from its neighbor by five small blocks (⅝"). Label this layout "Block Grouping B."

Design Exercises

Do each of the following design exercises on both of the layouts. Do each exercise on a piece of tracing paper laid over the construction-paper layout.

In Figures 132–133, you'll notice that the seams used to construct the traditional block-and-sashing strip layout touch the corners of each block.

Fig. 141.

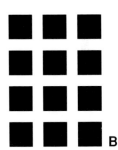

Fig. 142.

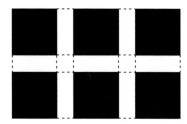

Fig. 143.

In our attempt to reach for the unexpected, *you will not be allowed to have any seams touch the corners of the blocks.* For the time being, suspend all judgment about piecing these designs in fabric. Think only of your attempt to design new, innovative layouts for your blocks.

EXERCISE 1: SINGLE HORIZONTAL AND VERTICAL LINES. With tracing paper over Block Grouping A, connect every adjacent pair of blocks with a single horizontal or vertical line, but do not let any of these lines touch a corner of a block. Then, still writing on tracing paper only, connect the blocks of Block Grouping B using the same restrictions.

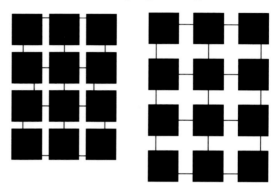

Fig. 144.

Notice that by using a single horizontal or vertical line to connect any two neighboring blocks, you've made it possible to create areas of color behind the blocks.

Fig. 145.

If you continue this concept out into the border, you create the illusion that the blocks are floating on a higher surface than the background. This is achieved by using the same fabric in the first border as the last fabric at the edge of the sashing strip between outer blocks.

Fig. 146.

EXERCISE 2: MULTIPLE HORIZONTAL AND VERTICAL LINES. Now you must connect any two adjacent blocks with more than one horizontal or vertical line—but again, none of these lines may touch the corner of a block.

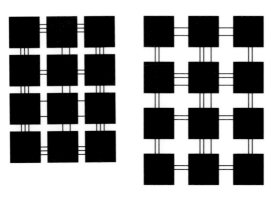

Fig. 147.

As you can see from Figure 147, using multiple horizontal and vertical lines allows you to create pathways of color between blocks.

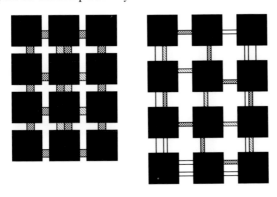

Fig. 148.

EXERCISE 3: SINGLE DIAGONAL LINES. Now you must connect any two adjacent blocks with a single diagonal line—it may slant in either direction (left to right or right to left), but there must be only one line between any two neighboring blocks, and the lines may not touch the corners of the blocks.

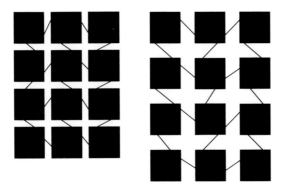

Fig. 149.

Some of the possible environments that these single diagonals could create appear in Figure 150.

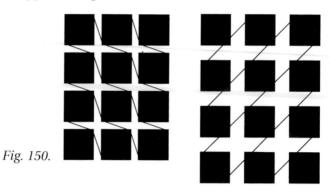

Fig. 150.

EXERCISE 4: MULTIPLE DIAGONAL LINES. Now you must connect any two adjacent blocks with two or more diagonal lines. They may slant in either direction (left to right or right to left)—and they may cross. But they still may not touch the corners of the blocks.

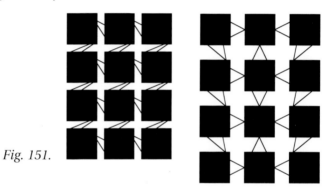

Fig. 151.

Crossed diagonals between blocks can serve as a mechanism for camouflaging where the block ends and the sashing strip begins. For example, in the block below, notice how the color from the block itself, when included in the adjacent sashing strip, gives the illusion that the block is "round" rather than square.

Fig. 152.

The elongated stars that form around the setting squares in the quilt Loma's Dutch Girls (below) illustrate another application of multiple diagonals in the sashing strips.

Loma's Dutch Girls by Margaret J. Miller, 1988, San Marcos, California, 62" x 98". The blocks in this quilt may be sixty years old, but all the rest of the materials are new. Blocks by Mrs. M. Allen Miller (mother of the quilt's present owner) and Mrs. Ben Wilson (friend of the family). Quilt designed, assembled, and hand quilted by Margaret J. Miller. Collection of Loma G. Hersom, San Jose, California.

The predictable way of drafting the stars would have been to draw the diagonal from the corner of the sashing strip at a 45° angle to the other side. But note how much more interesting it is to use another angle, and to start the star away from the corner of the block (Fig. 153).

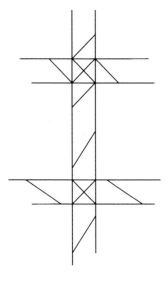

Fig. 153.

Still another approach to placing multiple diagonals connecting adjacent blocks is to place a ruler at the base of the grouping of blocks and use it to draw radiating lines across the blocks from either the corner or the center.

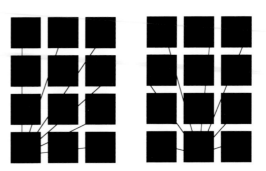

Fig. 154.

Draw the pencil line on the ruler's edge only in the sashing strips. (You may have to touch the corners of some of the blocks for this exercise.) This radiating effect in the sashing strips affords the possibility of grading color values in the background behind the blocks. Just two of many grading schemes are diagrammed in Figure 155.

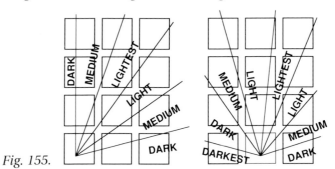

Fig. 155.

EXERCISE 5: DIAGONALS AND STRAIGHTS TOGETHER. When one is allowed to combine the previous exercises, any number of block backgrounds, or block environments, can emerge. Just a few suggestions appear in Figure 156.

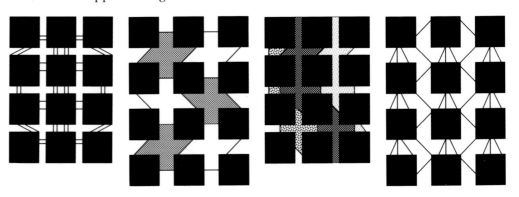

Fig. 156.

One may substitute another design element, such as a checkerboard, for sashing strips. This might be done in all the sashing strips of a quilt; in sashing strips one way only, either horizontally or vertically; or perhaps only in certain ones, as in the quilt Into Winter (below).

Note that the checkerboarded sashing strips are at the midlines of the quilt only, and that they darken in value outward, from the center of the quilt to the edges. The checkerboarding adds texture, and the change in value adds a subtle three-dimensional quality.

Checkerboards as sashing strips are used a bit differently in Allen's Teenage Quilt (page 58). Note that the checkerboarding is used in all the sashing strips outside of the medallion center of this quilt; however, in some areas the checkerboards are made of squares, in other areas, of rectangles.

Into Winter by Margaret J. Miller, 1981, San Marcos, California, 72" x 72". A study in how to vary sashing strips—in width, in design content, even by eliminating them in some areas of the quilt. Collection of the author.

Sashing strips can be designed specifically to enhance the motifs within the blocks they surround. The quilt Poppy II (below) is an especially pertinent example of this.

Poppy II by Margaret J. Miller, 1980, San Marcos, California, 72" x 93". The stained glass appliqué technique requires careful planning of sashing strips. The colors are unusually vibrant because of the narrow black line that surrounds each colored shape. Also, the blocks must be surrounded by a dark border so the viewer's eye is not led off each block in a scattered fashion. Collection of the author.

The appliqué blocks in this quilt are of a special type known as stained glass appliqué, a technique that enjoyed a brief surge of popularity in the early 1980s. The coloration of stained glass appliqué blocks is particularly vivid because of the thick black line surrounding each brightly colored shape within the block. These black lines are meant to represent the leading of stained glass windows, and tend to lead the eye shooting off the edge of the block unless it is surrounded by a dark border.

In Poppy II each block was framed with a 1" border of black fabric, and then the sashing strip was really only a 3" space between these bordered blocks. A special attempt was made to repeat the floral feeling of the blocks in the sashing strips but in a much more subtle fashion: the strip piecing of the sashing strips forms a geometric flower image in and around the setting squares (Fig. 157).

A special case of varying the content of the sashing strips is presented by the Amish Lights quilt (below).

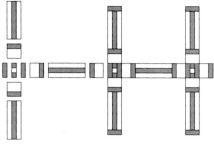

Fig. 157.

Amish Lights by Margaret J. Miller, 1989, Woodinville, Washington, 65" x 87". This quilt was begun with a set of twenty-five Amish-colored Churn Dash blocks. The reaching of the blue triangles from the edge of one block across the sashing strip and into the interior of the neighboring block adds a visual complexity to this pieced surface. Blocks made and top quilted by members of Canyon Quilters Guild, San Diego, California. Quilt raffled, fall 1990.

This quilt began with a set of twenty-five 9" Churn Dash blocks. A few of the blocks were sketched onto graph paper, separated by a 2" sashing strip as in Figure 158. The way to reach for the unexpected in this quilt was to have the blocks reach for each other with a shape that extended from one block into its neighbor. Thus, the strategy arose to draw a triangle whose base began 2" in from the corners of the blocks, and which extended into the neighboring block.

In the center of the quilt, the triangle was allowed to extend all the way to the center of the neighboring block; in the two rows flanking the

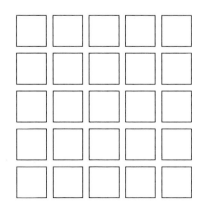

Fig. 158.

center row vertically, the triangle was allowed to extend only to the first major division line in the block. In the outer rows of blocks, the triangle extended only halfway across the center patch in the neighboring block.

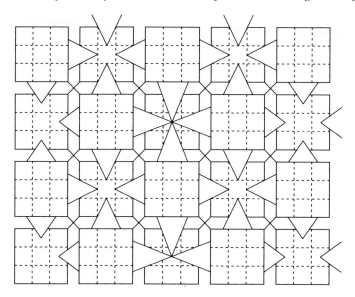

Fig. 159.

The crossed seams touching the corners of the blocks were added to allow different colors to be used in the lengthwise sashing strips than were used in the crosswise ones.

Now You See 'Em, Now You Don't: Eliminating Sashing Strips

Often in traditional quilt tops, it seems that the function of sashing strips is to isolate individual blocks. Another way of looking at the need for sashing strips is to consider them a support structure, a gridwork on which to hang a grouping of blocks.

This point of view eliminates the need to have a sashing strip separating every block from its neighbor, or to have sashing strips remain visible from one edge of the quilt all the way to the opposite edge. This is the philosophy behind the design of La Jolla Mauve (page 79). This quilt was a commission for a client who wanted a small quilt similar in feeling to Into Winter (page 75). The strong design elements of these two pieces are the checkerboarded areas, varied width of sashing strips, and in some areas, elimination of sashing strips altogether. When sashing strips (whether they be of solid fabric or textured as in the checkerboards) are interrupted by other shapes, a three-dimensional quality is infused into the quilt. Notice in La Jolla Mauve that the checkerboard sashing strips appear closer to the viewer than the dark ones, and both types seem closer than the wider mauve-colored strips. This is a simple mechanism for giving the visual impression of multiple layers in a quilt.

La Jolla Mauve by Margaret J. Miller, 1988, San Marcos, California, 49" x 49". This is the second piece in a series which explores variety among sashing strips in a single quilt. The relative color values used in the sashing strips accentuate the three-dimensional quality of this quilt. Collection of Pamela Anderson, Burlington, Washington.

Connecting Blocks with Diagonal Lines

One way to ensure that you reach for the unexpected in the arrangement of blocks in your quilt is to not allow yourself to line up blocks side by side or one below the other.

Martha Williams Friendship Quilt by Margaret J. Miller, 1986, San Marcos, California, 92" x 88". Blocks were made by members of the Evergreen Piecemakers quilt guild in Kent, Washington, in 1984 and were presented to Martha to thank her for her service as president of that guild. Movement of light to dark values in the background highlights certain areas of this quilt. Quilted by and in collection of Martha Williams, Kent, Washington.

To begin designing the Martha Williams Friendship Quilt (above), a single 9" block was drawn to scale on graph paper. Two lines were drawn from the left corners of the block upward diagonally across two graph-paper squares. The ends of these lines became the right side of the next block.

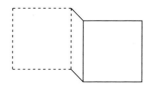

Fig. 160.

A single row of six blocks was completed in this fashion; but every time the upward diagonal lines were drawn, they were a different measurement: they crossed 2, 3, or 4 graph-paper squares diagonally.

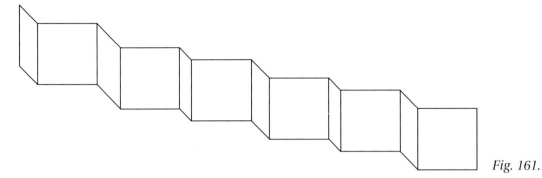

Fig. 161.

The positions of the succeeding rows of blocks were set by this first row.

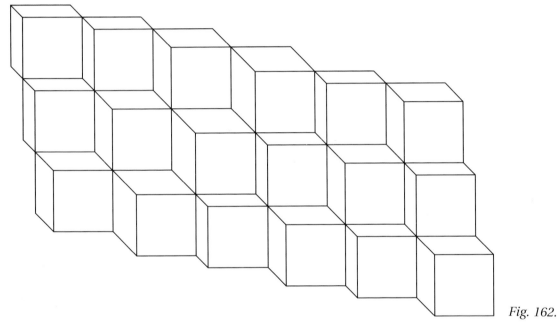

Fig. 162.

A rectangular inner border was added around the drawing for the quilt after all the blocks had been accounted for on graph paper, and any spaces not filled by blocks and sashing strips were filled in with a checkerboard pattern.

The friendship blocks in the Barbara McCroskey Friendship Quilt (below) are likewise connected by diagonal lines, but the first step in the design of this quilt was to create a three-dimensional box image behind each of her blocks. The houses then became the fronts of "moving boxes."

Barbara McCroskey Friendship Quilt by Margaret J. Miller, 1987, San Marcos, California, 70" x 83". The design of this quilt arose from making the House quilt block form the front of a three-dimensional open box, and then linking these boxes with diagonal lines that formed a cardboard ribbon. Blocks by friends of Barbara McCroskey, Poway, California. Quilted by and in collection of Barbara McCroskey, Carmel, Indiana.

These boxes were then connected by diagonal lines which formed a cardboard "ribbon" connecting all the houses. Significant to the three-dimensional look of this ribbon is the fact that whenever it slants from left to right, it is lighter beige in color than when it slants from right to left, giving the illusion that a light is shining from somewhere to the right of the quilt. Also, note that where the ribbon "turns" between rows of houses, it seems to overlap one of the borders of the quilt. This is a means of attaining the unexpected—by camouflaging where the body of the quilt stops and the border begins.

The quilt Block Party Trees (below) carries this idea of connecting blocks with diagonal lines a few steps further.

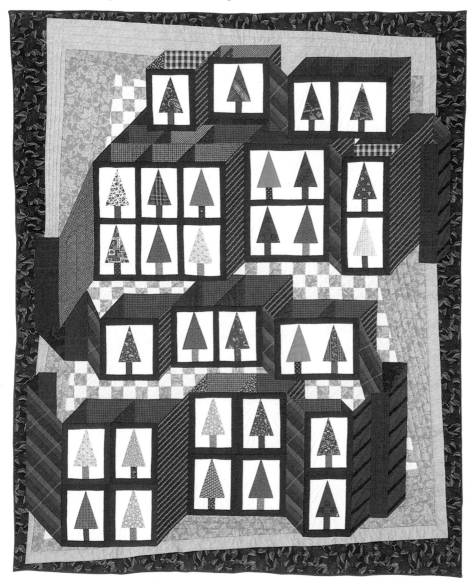

Block Party Trees by Margaret J. Miller, 1990, Woodinville, Washington, 74" x 90". These blocks were won as the "blocks of the month" for November 1989 at the Block Party Quilters guild of Kirkland, Washington. The block, The Alpine Tree, from Carolann Palmer's book Branching Out—Tree Quilts *(published by That Patchwork Place) was originally a square. But for this quilt, the square blocks were trimmed to form rectangles and placed in various groupings across the quilt. Note that the triple border is not parallel to the edges of the quilt. Blocks by members of Block Party Quilters guild. Collection of the author.*

In this quilt, groupings of blocks were put together as one unit, and these grouped blocks were connected with diagonal lines. This quilt dealt with the "bending" of the ribbon connector up to the next row of boxes, with multiple folds in the ribbon rather than a single fold as in the Barbara McCroskey Friendship Quilt.

All three of these quilts, the Martha Williams Friendship Quilt, the Barbara McCroskey Friendship Quilt, and the Block Party Trees quilt, were designed with pencil on graph paper, not with the method of cutting out construction-paper blanks to represent the quilt blocks. There is no substitute for doodling on graph paper to help new quilt arrangements "bubble to the surface." Keep all your graph-paper doodlings in your idea book, and refer to them from time to time. Over the years you may be surprised to notice how you return to certain motifs or quilt block arrangements again and again, if only on paper.

Fitting All Your Friends In; or, Oddly Shaped Blocks in One Quilt Top

Often, when one receives a group of friendship blocks, wins a group of blocks from a quilt guild or neighborhood sewing group, or tries to put together any group of blocks made by a number of different people, one has to deal with slight (or not so slight!) variations in block size. For example, though all blocks are supposed to be 12" finished, the sizes actually received may range from 11½" to 12¾", raw edge to raw edge. (Or perhaps they measure one figure in one direction, another in the other direction!) Hopefully, the following tips will help you keep your friendships with the block makers intact.

Multiple Sizes

One way to make each block uniform is to frame each one with a narrow band of fabric. This also helps the viewer focus on each block individually.

Cut a number of strips of fabric 1¾" wide. Trim given blocks to a square shape using a 15" Plexiglas square (these are available with multiple square sizes printed on them). It doesn't matter that each block will be a slightly different size square.

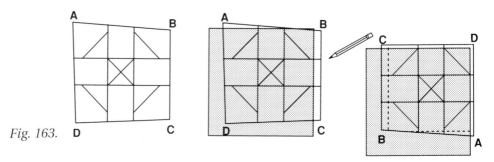

Fig. 163.

When possible, maintain a ¼" seam beyond points of stars or other obvious motifs within the block.

Sew 1¾" strips of fabric to opposite sides of a newly trimmed block; trim and press out.

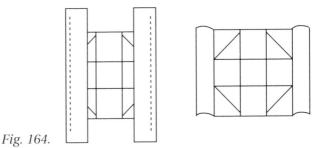

Fig. 164.

Sew 1¾" strips of fabric to remaining sides of block; trim and press out.

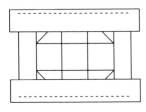 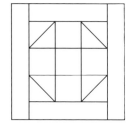

Fig. 165.

Make a posterboard template the size of the finished quilt block, according to the instructions in Appendix A (pages 158–161). Be sure to cut windows at the midpoints of the four sides of the template, to aid in lining up block seams. If the blocks have a motif that needs to be centered, perhaps a window cut in the center of the template as well as on the four sides would be helpful.

Turn block right side down, center template over block, and trace around template. This line is the sewing line, and in this case, it's being traced onto the border strips on each block.

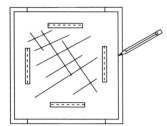

Fig. 166. Windows cut into block template help reveal edges of patchwork block underneath, and are especially useful when the block is not square.

Once all the blocks are a standard size, a construction-paper blank can be cut to scale for each block. These blanks can then be moved around a sheet of graph paper until a pleasing arrangement is discovered (see Blocks Offset, pages 30–39, for a detailed explanation of this process).

Glue down the construction-paper blanks, and place a sheet of tracing paper over them. On the tracing paper, you may draw in a number of seam arrangements that will make a meaningful environment for these blocks.

TRACING PAPER

Fig. 167.

This is the approach used to design the quilt Bernice's Baskets (page 36). The silhouette arrangements found on pages 34–35 are some of the block arrangements considered for this quilt.

Another way to incorporate multiple-size blocks into a quilt top is to use full- and half-size blocks, as in Springtime Memories I (below).

Springtime Memories I by Margaret J. Miller, 1990, Woodinville, Washington, 55" x 55". Blocks were made to the theme "Springtime Memories" by the customers of The Quilt Barn, Puyallup, Washington, in spring 1990. One of the blocks was divided into its four patches and the patches were used as individual quilt blocks. Quilt top temporarily in collection of Evelyn M. Griffin, The Quilt Barn, Puyallup, Washington, pending a drawing among block makers.

It is important to note that the 6" blocks in this quilt are not just miniature appliqués, but one of the 12" sampler blocks separated into four quarters. This combination is pleasing because the scale of the design within each block is the same. If the smaller blocks were miniatures, the effect might be jarring.

If you have a set of 12" sampler blocks, you might choose one or two of the Four Patch designs among them to subdivide and use as half-size blocks. These blocks could be duplicates of blocks in your given set, or other designs from your favorite patchwork pattern book.

Don't forget to consider these portions of blocks as diamond shapes as well as squares.

Fig. 168.

An added benefit to using partial pieced blocks is that often the partial blocks become asymmetrical, or directional. This helps to infuse a "flow" to the patterning of the blocks, and is a refreshing change from what can be unrelenting symmetry of traditional pieced blocks.

Also consider using half-blocks in combination with whole ones. Cut your photocopied blocks in half corner to corner to form triangles, or from side to side to form rectangles. Experiment with quilt layouts by gluing these shapes onto graph paper. Complete the design of the quilt surface by placing tracing paper over the glued block segments and using the block and blank approach to quilt design, described on pages 39–44. The dotted lines in the blocks in Figure 169 are design lines added to the original block and partial block layouts.

Block and Block Segments Used

Block Segments Used
Note that this pieced design has no whole blocks in it; it is made up of all block segments.

Fig. 169.

Blocks and Block Segments Used
Note the four different ways of completing the design in the corners. Some block lines have been eliminated, and the dotted lines are design lines.

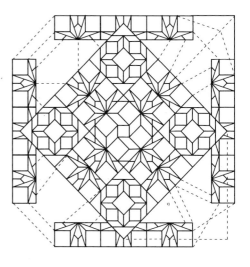

Below are only a few of many possible layouts for the subdivided Four Patch blocks, done in silhouette form. The elements considered are whole blocks (which could be a single pattern or sampler blocks), half-blocks, and quarter-blocks.

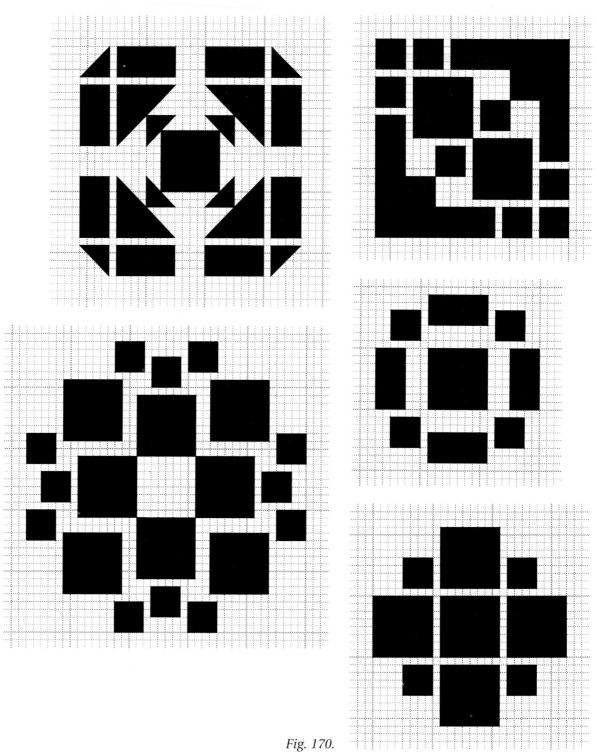

Fig. 170.

Multiple Shapes

It is not often that one would need to put many shapes into one quilt top, but occasionally the need does arise, as in the Friendship Quilters Guild Banner (page 62).

To come up with the arrangement for this quilt, the shapes were drawn to scale on graph paper, construction-paper blanks were made for each shape, and the arrangement of the blocks was derived. The piecing of the interior of this quilt was not a job for beginners, but it is presented here to prove that many assorted shapes can appear to belong together. The wide red inner border helps to prevent the scattered look these blocks might have without it.

SQUARES AND RECTANGLES. If your blocks have a centered motif surrounded by a lot of background, you have the option of incorporating variously shaped blocks into the same quilt. The Block Party Trees quilt (page 83) is based on such a block.

The basic block pattern is The Alpine Tree from page 37 of Carolann Palmer's book *Branching Out—Tree Quilts*. The tree motif is centered in the block; it extends to the top and bottom edges of the 8" block, but there are 2" of "free space" on either side of the tree. This opens up the possibilities of a) using the entire block as an 8" square, or b) cutting a margin off either side of the tree, making the block into a rectangle.

    OR

Fig. 171.

A block with such a simple design begs to be used in groupings: either single or multiple rows, or boxed groupings as diagrammed below.

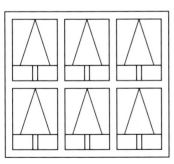 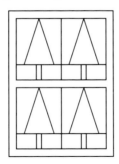

Fig. 172.

This concept is also useful if you have a small number of blocks which are not enough for the size quilt top you would like to make. For example, if you have four appliqué blocks, they could be arranged as follows, and smaller rectangular blocks could be designed, incorporating some of the motifs of the larger blocks, to fill in the spaces (Fig. 173).

SQUARES AND DIAMONDS. Certain motifs, such as baskets, have a definite direction to them; some need to be positioned as squares and some as diamonds. When you must combine these two shapes in the same quilt, your ability to maneuver graph paper becomes a crucial talent.

Fig. 173.

In Ann Albertson's Friendship Quilt (below), there was a significant number of blocks that had to be put on point, or in a diamond position.

Ann Albertson's Friendship Quilt by Margaret J. Miller, 1984, San Marcos, California, 77" x 77". This example of numerous square and diamond-shaped blocks in the same pieced surface features new angles in the border which give the illusion one is looking through a circular opening at the grouping of blocks.

Blocks made by members of Friendship Quilters Guild of Poway, California, and others in tribute to Ann Albertson for her years of effort nurturing quiltmaking in the San Diego area. Collection of Ann M. Albertson, Escondido, California.

On graph paper, the blocks were drawn out in a traditional manner, with 2" sashing strips separating the 6" blocks. Seam lines were drawn in because it was hoped that a "weaving" of the sashing strips could be incorporated into this central area.

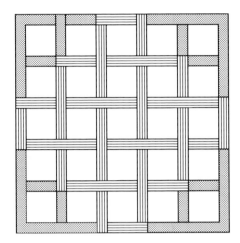

Fig. 174.

This drawing of the quilt center was then cut out, rotated so that it formed a diamond, and glued lightly onto another piece of graph paper. A border was constructed around the diamond by counting four graph-paper squares out from its north, south, east, and west points, and joining those new points to form a border diamond.

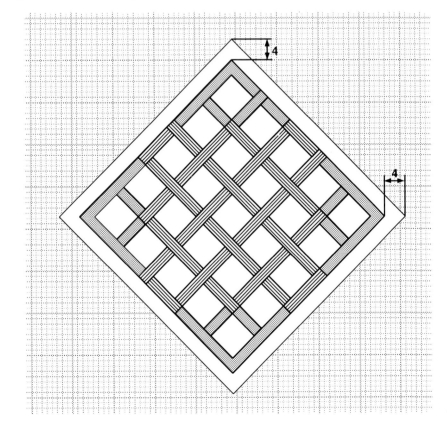

Fig. 175.

The balance of the quilt could then be sketched in around the central grouping of blocks. The square blocks were sketched in first, then the lines "behind" them to form a cohesive pieced surface. The dotted lines in Figure 176 are seam lines that must be added to assemble this quilt.

Notice that there are only two lines (lines AB and CD) in this layout which form other than 90° or 45° angles with the edge of the quilt. Line AB gives the illusion that there is a concave diamond bordering the central grouping of blocks; line CD makes it appear you are looking through a circular opening at a special collection of friendship blocks.

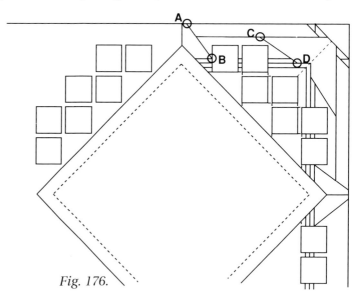

Fig. 176.

In this early stage of designing such a quilt, one could sketch either four different ideas off the four edges of the central diamond, or put a piece of tracing paper over this graph-paper assemblage and be able to sketch out many more ideas.

Many quiltmakers find using tracing paper to be a freeing experience—because if a design doesn't work, you can just lift off the tracing paper and throw it away—and not engage in any laborious erasing. Putting a sheet of tracing paper over the basic block grouping sometimes frees you to sketch more ideas than you would try otherwise. As a final quilt plan begins to crystallize, you can draft more carefully on the graph paper itself (without tracing paper over it).

The quilt Bernice's Baskets (page 36) also involves squares and diamonds, but in the reverse position—the diamonds are on the outside, the squares (of which there are only six in the group of thirty-nine total blocks) are in the center. As has been previously discussed, this quilt was first designed using construction-paper blanks (see pages 34–35). Tracing paper was then placed over the construction-paper blanks to draw in seam lines to make a harmonious whole.

Since the majority of the blocks in this quilt are diamonds, the entire quilt could be designed with the graph paper turned on an angle. The inner area of the quilt was formed by drawing a line from corner to corner through graph-paper squares, rather than along any given graph-paper line. The dotted lines in Figure 177 are the only design lines in Bernice's Baskets that had to be drawn corner-to-corner on the graph paper.

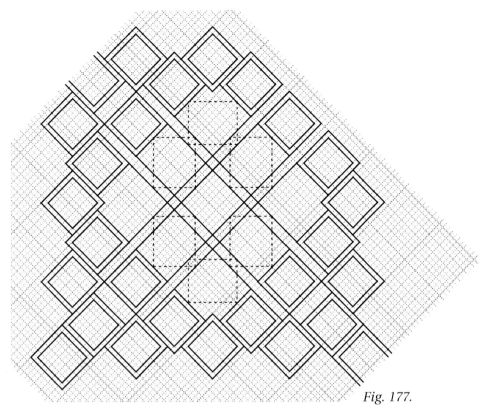

Fig. 177.

Note that in the center of the quilt the square blocks overlap the sashing strips which come in from the corner blocks. Where they overlap the white sashing strips, lighter values of the block frames are used to generate the illusion of transparency.

Detail of center blocks in Bernice's Baskets showing corners of blocks overlapping sashing strips

Sue Connoley has used the diamonds in her quilt Fiesta Rose (below) in quite a different manner: the diamonds set the width of not only the sashing strips between the square blocks, but also the wide border around them. The unique location of the diamonds in relation to the squares makes it appear that the squares are on a turntable, and are about to be set in motion.

Fiesta Rose by Susan M. Connoley, 1990, Tacoma, Washington, 66" x 66". The use of "setting diamonds" instead of "setting squares," to mark where the sashing strips meet, sets off a real design adventure in this piece. Note the numerous new angles used and the carrying of design lines all the way to the border, though they may be interrupted by another shape. Collection of the quiltmaker, Gig Harbor, Washington.

This quilt appears to illustrate one way to connect square blocks with diagonal lines (pages 80–83), but in this case the diagonal connector line is the side of a small diamond-shaped block. Also, note the role of the diagonal lines in the central sashing strips—they are angles very different from the 45° angles of the diamonds against the squares, and as such they add much motion to the quilt in general.

Three other quilts in this book are also examples of incorporating square and diamond shapes into a single quilt surface: Allen's Teenage Quilt (page 58), Gathering Basket: A Signature Quilt (page 60), and United Against All Odds (page 115).

The Borders

Gone are the days when the most appropriate border for every quilt was a "slab" of fabric 6" wide surrounding the rigid grouping of blocks. In our effort to reach for the unexpected in a quilt, the border becomes one with the pathways between the blocks to create a setting or an environment for the blocks, rather than serving to hem them in or surround them like a poorly chosen frame for a fine oil painting.

Camouflaging Where the Blocks Stop and the Border Begins

One of the chief ways to reach for the unexpected in border design is to camouflage where the grouping of blocks stops and the border begins—again, making the viewer consider the entire surface of the quilt, not just a block or two. This factor is more important in some pieced surfaces than others.

We have already seen this principle in action in two quilts, wherein the blocks overlap one or more of the borders of the quilt: Block Party Trees (page 83) and the Barbara McCroskey Friendship Quilt (page 82). To see how this is actually planned out in a quilt, we'll take a close look at Rachel Kincy Clark's Friendship Quilt (page 96). The motif idea of Rachel's quilt was to make the quilt blocks the fronts of happily distorted boxes, and to suspend these boxes on barber poles. Once the central motif was drafted to scale on graph paper, the outer edge of the quilt was placed 4" beyond the highest and lowest point of the design, and 3" beyond the most extreme point on either side of the quilt. (Only the upper left portion of the quilt is shown below.)

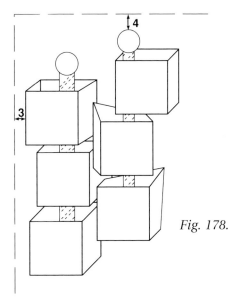

Fig. 178.

Rachel Kincy Clark's Friendship Quilt by Margaret J. Miller, 1989, San Marcos, California, 83" x 93". The blocks were first drawn on graph paper as the fronts of happily distorted three-dimensional boxes; the barber poles were then drawn in where appropriate in the design. The pole bases were constructed using eight shades of hand-dyed fabric, thus emphasizing the three-dimensional look. Blocks by early quilting friends of Rachel Kincy Clark. Collection of Rachel Kincy Clark, Watsonville, California.

The border on this quilt was in three parts: a wide (5") outer border, a 2" narrow one, then a 5" checkerboard.

To draw the line delineating the inner edge of the checkerboard border, a ruler was placed across the drawing of the quilt 7" in from the edge of the quilt. The line was actually drawn on the paper only in areas where the motifs from the center of the quilt did not interfere with it.

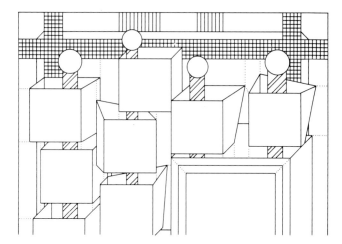

Fig. 179.

The 5" checkerboard border was then filled in.

By placing the ruler parallel to the outer edge of the checkerboard and 2" away from it, the narrow border could be drawn in: again, it was drawn only in the areas where motifs from the center of the quilt were not already drafted. This mode of drafting is actually drawing in the border "behind" the quilt.

Another quilt in which the main blocks of the quilt seem to overlap several of the borders is the Thompson Retirement Quilt (below).

Thompson Retirement Quilt by Margaret J. Miller, 1983, San Marcos, California, 52" x 52". Blocks by Thompson children using liquid embroidery pens on muslin. Quilt was presented to parents Arthur and Isabel Thompson as a surprise at a retirement dinner honoring Dr. Thompson's thirty years of teaching and research at the University of Maryland. Collection of Dr. and Mrs. Arthur H. Thompson, College Park, Maryland.

The pieced border of this quilt was sketched on graph paper ahead of time, and chosen for its simplicity and divisibility by an even number. One corner section of the pieced border (between the red bars) was drafted so that the points of the central diamond would extend beyond it on all four sides.

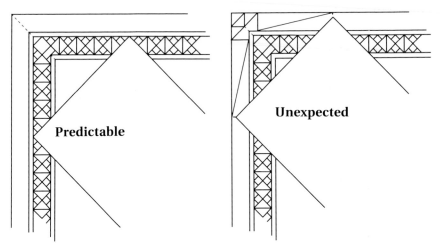

Predictable

Unexpected

Fig. 180.

Simple Shapes as Borders

Sometimes the simplest motifs can be used in interesting ways to create a geometric field around the quilt. Consider basic motifs like checkerboards, rows of equilateral triangles, diamonds, or parallelograms, and see how you can reach for the unexpected by changing their size, shape, spacing, location, and direction. We will examine each of these properties individually, using the flying geese pattern (rows of triangles) as an example. In all the drawings that follow, the solid lines are design lines, but the dotted lines indicate additional seams necessary to assemble these borders.

SIZE: big or little, short or tall. Traditionally, flying geese triangles are all the same size and width. But how much more interesting it is to alter their height, their width, or perhaps both dimensions at once, as they march along the edge of your quilt.

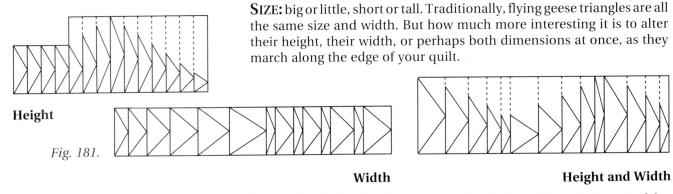

Height

Fig. 181.

Width

Height and Width

SHAPE: Traditionally, flying geese triangles have the point (apex) of the triangle at the midpoint of the opposite side of the rectangle in which they reside. Here's what happens if we move the apex of the triangle along that side:

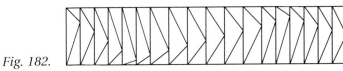

Fig. 182.

An example of this movement is in the quilt Starry, Starry Sampler (page 27); the flying geese that help frame the center of the quilt change subtly in shape as they march from one block to the next (Fig. 183).

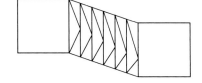

Fig. 183.

SPACING: near and far. Normally, flying geese triangles touch each other, but perhaps they could be spaced farther from one another in some cases.

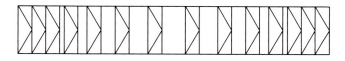

Fig. 184.

One option you have is to add design lines to connect the isolated "geese." Just three of numerous graphic strategies for accomplishing this are diagrammed below.

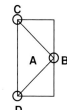

Anatomy of a Flying Goose
A = goose triangle
B = goose beak
C, D = wing tips

Fig. 185.

a) In each blank separator space, find what would be the goose beak; connect that point with the wing tips of the goose to the left of the separator space.

b) Connect goose beak with end of second division line to right. This line, when drawn, is interrupted by a triangular goose.

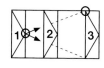

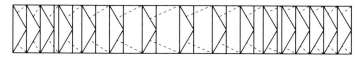

Fig. 186.

c) Wing tips of goose 3 are lined up with beak of goose 1, skipping goose 2. Connect design points with ruler, but draw line only from goose 3 to goose 2. Repeat along border.

The close-together spacing could be taken to the extreme through overlapping. More than one visual effect can be achieved by overlapping flying geese triangles.

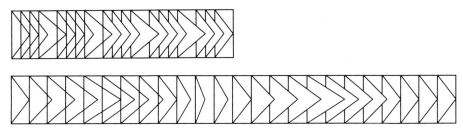

Fig. 187.

In the diagrams above, the triangles on the left have all design lines drawn completely. On the right, some lines are interrupted by a neighboring goose triangle.

LOCATION: up and down. Normally, flying geese triangles are placed in a line at the same level. But they could be placed higher or lower in relation to each other, to create an undulating border.

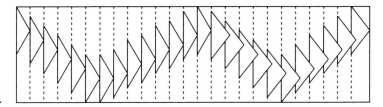

Fig. 188.

An example of this kind of border can be seen in A Quilt of Kentucky Friendship (page 101). In this quilt, the undulating nature of the flying geese border is accentuated with the use of much darker fabric on one side of the geese than on the other.

DIRECTION: pointing left or right, up or down. This is a crucial aspect of border design using triangles, because of the number of places at which a change in direction can occur: at the midpoint of the border, at the corners, or continuously around the edge of the quilt.

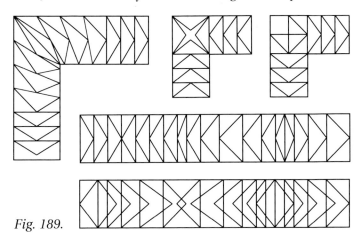

Fig. 189.

A Quilt of Kentucky Friendship by Margaret J. Miller, 1988, San Marcos, California, 101" x 114". The dominant design device in this quilt is the flying geese traditional pattern, which forms the medallion around the central block, as well as part of the border. Blocks by Kentucky quilting friends of Pat Scoville; designed and assembled by Margaret J. Miller as a birthday present for Pat; quilted by Pat Scoville. Collection of Pat Scoville, Westlake Village, California.

Fig. 190.

The medallion around the large block in A Quilt of Kentucky Friendship is formed by flying geese triangles that vary in height and direction. Their dimensionality is further accentuated by the alternating light and dark triangles (Fig. 190).

Rows of Blocks as Borders

Some quilts do not require any different geometric arrangement other than a final row of blocks to complete the quilt. In the Loma's Dutch Girls quilt (page 73), and Allen's Teenage Quilt (page 58), the final row of blocks functions as a border.

In the Loma's Dutch Girls quilt, notice that the background area of the block is darker in one half of the block (the half closest to the outer edge of the quilt); this in itself helps to form a border. This was done purposely because the bed for which the quilt was designed does not allow for a wider or longer quilt, eliminating the possibility of adding successive strips of fabric for further bordering.

Another example of a row of blocks forming a border is Starry, Starry Sampler (page 27). In this border, the traditional block has been distorted, and the closeness of the distortion to the outer edges of the quilt becomes an effervescent ending to the quilt.

Completing Motifs

In quilts where there are no sashing strips separating the blocks, one can readily identify certain design motifs—diamonds, triangles, stars, and the like—that are interrupted by the edge of an outer block. Reaching for the unexpected in border design for such quilts demands that certain of these motifs be completed in the border.

To reach for the unexpected, it is important to complete the motifs in one way in one part of the border, in another way in other areas of the border. For example, the diamond motifs in the layout below could be completed partway across the border strips on the north and south sides of the quilt, perhaps, and extend to the absolute edge of the quilt on the east and west sides. Star motifs are also amenable to building interesting borders around groupings of blocks.

From Block Elements to Borders

Go back to your favorite checkerboard pattern from the Blocks Together chapter. Find additional photocopies of the blocks used in that
checkerboard.

Cut the extra photocopies of the pattern apart in different ways to see
what design motifs you can discover. There are a number of ways you
could cut the block apart, as seen below:

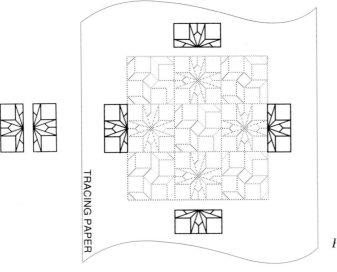

Fig. 191.

Place a sheet of tracing paper over your checkerboard pattern and place
a couple of the elements from your cut-apart block randomly near the
edges of your checkerboard "quilt." The elements may touch the edge
of the quilt or they may be farther away from it.

TRACING PAPER

Fig. 192.

Now draw design lines to connect the elements with the body of your blocks; thus, the element cut out of the block has been the jumping-off place for border design.

Note that you can reach for the unexpected by placing the elements nearer the quilt at the sides, and farther away at the top and bottom.

Or perhaps you will "plug in" the cut-apart block elements at the corners of the quilt.

If you have trouble with this technique, perhaps you need to change the scale of the element you are trying to use to spawn your border. Draw it a little larger or a little smaller, and see if that modification leads to a more properly proportioned border.

Extending Design Lines

The technique of extending design lines from the blocks out into the borders (a technique that was an integral part of the block and blank approach to quilt design, pages 39–44), is another useful method for designing a border setting for quilt blocks. This can be done in a regular rhythm all around the edges of the quilt, as in the Amish Lights quilt (page 77). But watch for chances to extend lines that will not meet in a predictable way, or to fill shapes created in the border with more than one fabric.

In the border of Amish Lights, for example, the crossed design lines inside the setting squares of the sashing strips were extended until they hit the outer edge of the quilt. This produced a very regular border, but the diagonals did not meet at a point at the quilt's edge. Moreover, the illusion was created that the border consisted of the last sashing strip plus the border, housed in a hexagonal shape.

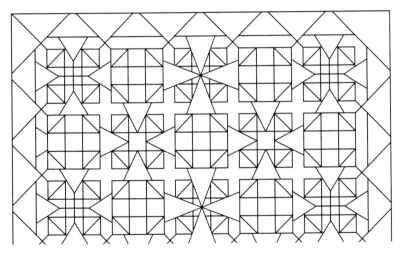

Fig. 193.

The border provided a setting for the blocks by being made of significantly darker fabrics than those in the quilt.

Cutaways

When you work with rows of blocks that are offset (see Blocks Offset, pages 30–39), you have the option of cutting away a portion of that part of the block extending beyond the main body of blocks (Fig. 194).

Fig. 194.

You can then draw the border lines in such a way that they are interrupted by the shapes that extend beyond the main body of blocks. This makes the border appear to be behind the motif that stands out beyond the main body of blocks (Fig. 195).

This technique is used in the quilt Ice of Iris (below). The block is rectangular; each row is offset by one-half block.

Fig. 195.

Ice of Iris by Margaret J. Miller, 1984, San Marcos, California, 36" x 47". The dominant design feature of this quilt is that rows of rectangular blocks are offset by one-half block. Portions of the outer blocks were cut away, and the border lines drawn in behind the block parts which remained. Collection of Marjorie R. Crist, Santa Rosa, California.

You may choose to have the cutaways overlap the border on two edges only, as in Ice of Iris, or on all four edges as in the mock-up on page 107.

Changing the Angle

Traditionally, borders have formed a rectangular frame around a given grouping of blocks; but when you focus on reaching for the unexpected in border design, you might change the angles involved in that rectangular border in a number of ways.

Rectangle Askew

In the Block Party Trees quilt (page 83), the edges of the blocks are parallel to the sides of the quilt, but the triple border is askew. This was achieved by literally picking out corner points within the border that did not line up in the traditional way.

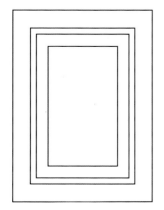 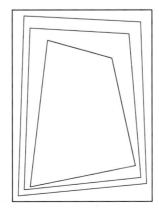

Fig. 196.

The blocks were first drawn on graph paper in their folded ribbon format (see Connecting Blocks with Diagonal Lines, pages 80–83). The outer edge of the quilt was then drawn by counting out four small graph-paper squares from the outermost block line north and south, and counting out two small graph-paper squares from the outermost block line east and west.

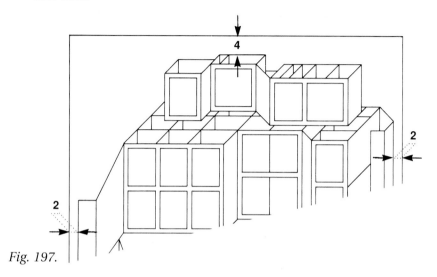

Fig. 197.

Then, design points were established to mark the corners of the next border in toward the center of the quilt. A design line was drawn between each pair of adjacent corner design points. This line was interrupted by any block motif already drawn on the graph paper.

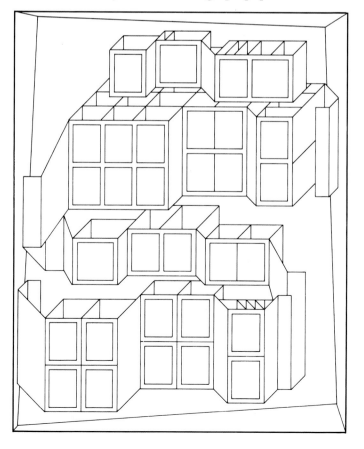

Fig. 198.

This process was repeated two more times—I determined design points for the corners, then connected them with a design line that was interrupted by the central motif. This completed a triple border with a center, all of which appeared to have a grouping of blocks superimposed upon it.

Continuous Ribbon Borders

Another effective way of framing a block grouping is to connect design points that will create a symmetrical yet irregular ribbonlike shape around and behind the blocks. This ribbon frame is most effective if it is created by drawing angles unlike any angles appearing within the blocks themselves.

For example, the quilt San Diego Friends I (cover and below) was created by first drawing the block arrangement and the diamond shape behind the blocks on graph paper.

San Diego Friends I by Margaret J. Miller, 1990, Woodinville, Washington, 66" x 84". Farewell blocks by quilting friends of Margaret J. Miller, part of a collection of fifty blocks set into a three-quilt series. Among the fifty blocks, there was only one which had to be used as a diamond; it appears in this quilt. Quilted by Pat Scoville, Ann Albertson, Patty B. Smith, Jan Inouye, and Judy Mathieson. Collection of the author.

The corner diagonal lines were established by counting eight squares horizontally and eight squares vertically from the corners.

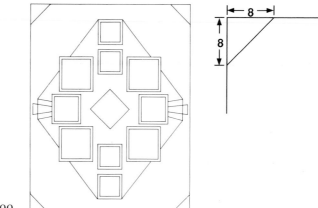

Fig. 199.

The ribbons along the sides of the quilt were drawn in first, by connecting the diagonal line DE with the top (and later the bottom) edge of block A. This was done by connecting points D and F first, then E and G: the lines were interrupted by block B and by the diamond shape around the blocks.

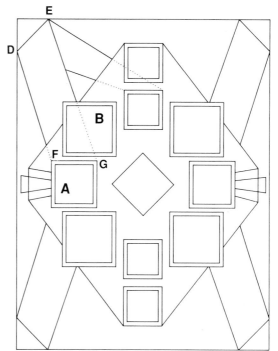

Fig. 200.

The ribbons along the top were drawn next, by connecting the corner diagonal line with the top edge of block C (at the bottom of the quilt, the diagonal is connected with the bottom edge of block C). The lines were determined by lining up a ruler to join points D and H, then points E and I; but the lines drawn here are much shorter because they are interrupted not only by the diamond shape, but also by the portion of the ribbon drawn in Figure 200.

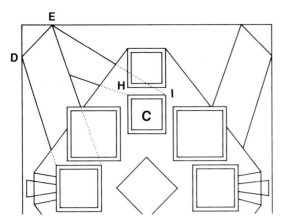

Fig. 201.

When this quilt was still only a diagram on paper, it was assumed that these ribbon paths would be cut from single fabrics (though the plan was to use light, medium, and dark values of a given color). However, as the quilt was actually cut out and put up on the design wall, it became evident that these shapes were too large in scale to properly frame the center of this quilt. Therefore, the ribbon paths were broken up into flying geese segments. Notice how much more effective it is to have extra fabric filling the triangular spaces between the "wing tips" of the flying geese, than to use only one fabric in that area.

A similar approach was used to design Springtime Memories I (page 86). The center of the quilt was drafted with block lines on graph-paper lines first, then the graph paper was turned on point to complete the designing of the border.

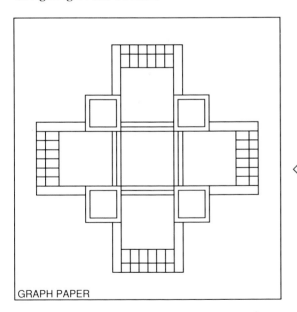

GRAPH PAPER

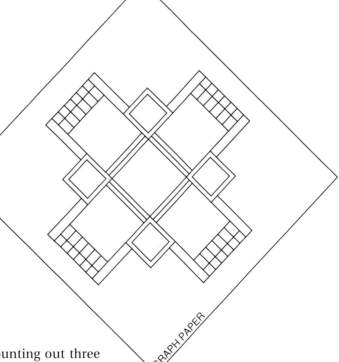

GRAPH PAPER

Fig. 202.

The outer edge of the quilt was determined by counting out three graph-paper diamonds from the outermost corners of the block sashings. Once the edge of the quilt was drawn, the corner lines AB were established by counting in four graph-paper diamonds from the corner, and drawing a diagonal line (which is eight squares long). The ends of this diagonal line are connected with the corners of the blocks at the center of the top, bottom, and sides of the quilt. However, notice that this line (AC and BD) is interrupted by a shape already in place from the center arrangement of blocks. The corner shape was then filled in with more diagonals to create a graceful overlapping effect; this was later accentuated by using light, medium, and dark color values. Again, note the effectiveness of creating the illusion that one shape is overlapped by another. This is achieved by drawing lines which are interrupted by shapes already in place.

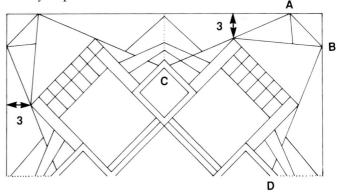

Fig. 203.

The same design procedure was used in Bernice's Baskets (page 36). However, the shapes that filled the quilt's corners were more complex in both design and fabric composition.

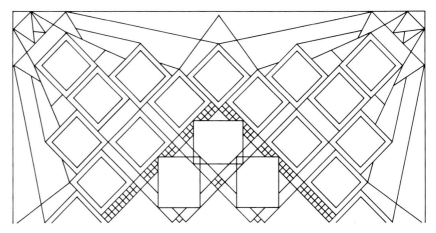

Fig. 204.

Seeing Circles

The same gentle angles surrounding the blocks can form a softly circular frame around them, instead of an angular one, as in the three preceding examples. In The Hales Quilt (page 113), for example, two overlapping inverted triangles were drawn at the center of the edges of the quilt; these triangles were overlapped by the center quilt block on all sides.

The Hales Quilt by Margaret J. Miller, 1988, San Marcos, California, 61" x 61". A number of design challenges were presented by this quilt, made of contest blocks from The Quilt Shop in Stanwood, Washington. Among those challenges was the odd number of blocks (thirteen), the pale values in colors used, and designing a gentle setting to enhance the nature of the blocks. Note the use of transparency as the eye travels from corner to corner of the quilt, across the middle side blocks. Collection of Betty Charette, Aberdeen, Washington.

Design points were located by counting graph-paper squares up the sides of the corner blocks from their inner corners. These corner blocks were further surrounded by a narrow frame that was interrupted by the actual corner motif. The corner motif was developed by sketching on graph paper, and designed to be a continuation of the flying geese motif that connected the center grouping of blocks with the corner blocks.

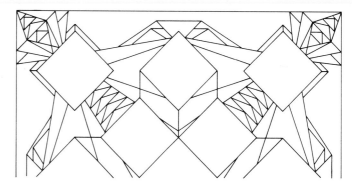

Fig. 205.

An even stronger circular feeling is generated by only two angled lines in the borders of Ann Albertson's Friendship Quilt (page 90). The design points which created the angles were devised not by using a protractor or any fancy geometry, but by counting squares on graph paper.

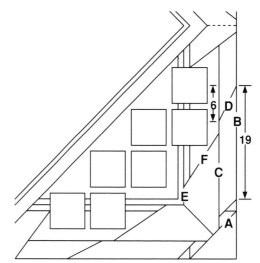

Fig. 206.

The design points marking the beginning and ending of the diagonal lines were merely a certain number of inches from each corner. This simple graphic mechanism gives the illusion that the viewer is looking at this special collection of friendship blocks through a round window.

Sara Quattlebaum, in her quilt United Against All Odds (page 115) has also used soft angles to create the illusion of not only circles but ovals.

United Against All Odds by Sara Quattlebaum, 1990, Olympia, Washington, 84" x 84". A number of subtleties bring surprises to viewers of this quilt top. Note the contrast between very bright and very subdued blocks; the rust fabrics echo from the central oval to the outer corner units. The outer blocks blend almost invisibly with the checkerboarded circle surrounding the total grouping of treasured squares from Sara's early quiltmaking classes. Collection of the quiltmaker.

The oval along the center vertical spine of the quilt is formed by connecting design points at the corners of blocks, a line which is interrupted by other blocks.

Fig. 207.

The blue checkerboard "circle" is a combination of connecting design points and extending that line until it intersects with a like line from the adjacent side of the quilt (Fig. 208).

A circular shape can be suggested by very few design lines in a quilt. In the Thompson Retirement Quilt (page 97), the only angles in the quilt that are not 45° or 90° are created by the two seams forming the outer edges of the yellow triangles in the border. Notice how much of a softening effect just two design lines can have on a total quilt design.

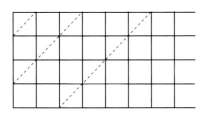

Fig. 208.

Angles Creating Shadows on Checkerboards

One may wish to reach for the unexpected in very predictable places, such as in a checkerboard border around a quilt. This can be achieved by superimposing seam lines at new angles over the checkerboard and using two different systems of color in the spaces between the diagonal lines. The predictable approach to combining diagonals and checkerboards would be to draw the diagonals corner to corner as in Figure 209.

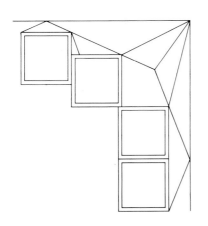

Fig. 209.

To reach for the unexpected, draw the checkerboard, then lay your ruler across it at such an angle that the ruler does not touch any corners of the checkerboard.

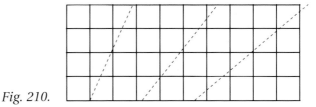

Fig. 210.

This approach can be further refined if you start with an irregularly spaced checkerboard and again place the ruler so that it touches no corners.

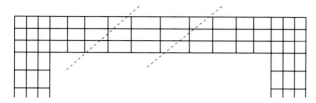

Fig. 211.

This border style appears in the quilt Sea Route (below).

Sea Route by Margaret J. Miller, 1986, San Marcos, California, 59" x 59". Curved lines from the interior of this quilt are enhanced by the lines dividing the green and brown checkerboards in the border. The light-to-dark color scheme is carried from the quilt center out into the border. The strategy of light on the left to darker on the right in the body of the quilt is carried out differently in different shapes within the block (for example, note the value progression in the green triangles, then in the triangles "behind" the strip-pieced parallelograms). Collection of the author.

To construct the 6" wide border, two different checkerboards were sewn: one green/white and the other rust/brown. First, the border was drawn out full size on graph paper (including checkerboard seam lines). A ruler was placed over this checkerboard in the manner described above, and then the three simple template shapes were made from this drawing and pieces cut from the appropriate fabric combinations.

Template A   **Template B**   **Template C**

Color Strategies: Some General Notes

Extensive color theory as applied to fabric selection for quilts is beyond the scope of this book. However, I would like to pass along some general rules of thumb that beginning quiltmakers should find helpful in their use of color.

Attitude and Environment

1. If you are the type of quiltmaker who chants "But I can't use color," or "I just can't put fabrics together," your first step is to adjust your attitude. Whenever I hear students saying this I am reminded of the old proverb, "If you think you can or you think you can't . . . you're right!"
2. "Design is a visual experience, not an intellectual one." I heard and wrote down this expression early on in my development as a quiltmaker, and it's one I've called to mind again and again. It pertains as much to color as it does to design. You can pace the floor in the fabric shop as long as you want, agonizing about choosing a fourth color while you carry three heavy bolts in your arms; but until you get home and start cutting that fabric and looking at it on a design wall in proportionate bits, you cannot predict what the color is going to look like in your quilt.
3. In our everyday environment, we cannot focus on one color without seeing it in the context of its color surroundings. The same thing happens with quilts: you never know what color a fabric will be in a quilt until you see how much of it will appear in a given area, and what fabric color—and how much of that—surrounds it.
4. Since we cannot mix color like an oil painter can, we must collect color in the form of bits of fabric, so that we have a palette of color to draw from for any one quilt. This collecting of color takes a lifetime—not one or two trips to the local fabric store.
5. Learning to use color takes time and observation and practice. You can read all the art books you want, but until you try to put those art exercises into practice with real fabric again and again, you will not learn how to use color in quilts.
6. If you use only three fabrics in a given project, it may be obvious that one of those three fabrics doesn't go well with the other two. If, on the other hand, you use thirty fabrics in a project, the eye will blend all those colors together, and no one fabric will stand out as a misfit. Running out of fabric can be a blessing to a quiltmaker—because it forces the quiltmaker to come up with two or three fabrics to create the same value in a given area of a quilt (see Richness of Surface, pages 127–130).

7. The best way to evaluate color is to create your quilt on a vertical surface, not a horizontal one, and to distance yourself from that surface. I use two 4' x 8' Celotex (or soundboard) panels covered by lengths of flannel fabric. This way, I can cut out a piece of fabric, put it up on the design wall (where it sticks to the fuzzy surface without needing to be pinned), and stand back from it to evaluate the relative success of my choice. To create more distance from the design wall, you may use a reducing glass, a pair of binoculars (peer through the wrong end of them to make the image seem farther away), or the viewfinder on your camera. The viewfinder does not get you as far away from the image as a reducing glass does, but at least the camera masks all visual stimuli in the room except for the quilt surface being created.

8. To use color well and effectively in quilts, one must begin to think of fabrics not as color names but as values—light, light medium, medium, medium dark, and dark.

9. It is interesting for the quiltmaker and the viewer to move values across the quilt—from light to dark as the eye moves from left to right, or top to bottom, or corner to corner.

Specific Color Strategies

In order to simplify the process of learning to move values across the quilt, below are a number of specific color strategies for you to try in a quilt pattern you have already used, or in one which you have designed but not yet worked up in fabric.

Remember that one way to "work in a series" is to take a single graphic mechanism, such as a pieced quilt design, and apply a number of different color strategies to that design. In the following section, a quilt of traditional design and one of more abstract design will be used to illustrate this principle.

It is helpful to realize that we are not so much assigning colors to certain areas of the quilt as we are *sprinkling light across the surface.* With this in mind, we will be talking about light, medium, and dark values rather than specific color names (red, blue, teal, and so on).

Notice in the following examples that the areas labeled "light" may have a few medium or dark fabrics. If only light fabrics were used in the areas labeled "light," only medium values in the areas marked "medium," and only dark values in "dark" areas, the result would be a very awkward-looking quilt. All light fabrics in the light area, for example, would make that area look washed out, or like a photograph taken with a flash gun at too close range. It is a few mediums and darks sprinkled into the light area which really makes the lights shine; likewise, a few mediums in the dark area can make darks look almost like velvet.

Horizontal Bands of Light

In this strategy, the illusion is that there is a fluorescent tube placed near the top edge of the quilt. Therefore, the lightest values are at the top, gradually darkening to medium values in the middle, with the darkest values of fabrics used at the bottom edge of the quilt (Fig. 212).

LIGHT
MEDIUM
DARK

Fig. 212.

Vertical Spine of Light

Perhaps your lightest values will form a vertical line down the center of the quilt, flanked by medium values, with the darkest values falling along the side edges (Fig. 213).

DARK	MEDIUM	LIGHT	MEDIUM	DARK

Fig. 213.

Diagonal Shaft of Light

Fig. 214.

If this same shaft of light were to extend corner to corner, the lights would be placed in a narrow, perhaps pointed, oval from corner to corner; these patches filled with light values would be surrounded by medium and then dark pieces (Fig. 214).

Crossed Shafts of Light

Fig. 215.

To carry the above one step further, perhaps you would take two corner-to-corner light beams and cross them over the center of the quilt (Fig. 215). This effect would be most interesting if one shaft were red, one shaft were blue. Where they cross in the center, use of burgundy, purple, maroon, and the like would give the illusion that you were looking through one shaft of light at the other one.

Centered Lights

You may try to create the illusion of a spotlight focused on the center of your quilt. There are two ways to create this illusion (Fig. 216). One is to follow block lines to delineate where the lights stop and the mediums begin, and likewise where the mediums stop and the darks begin. For example, the center four blocks in the quilt might be primarily light in value; the next ring of blocks may be medium in value, and the final ring may be darkest of all.

Fig. 216.

Or, a more general plan may be followed, where the lights, mediums, and darks flow across block lines into generalized rings of increasingly dark values from the center to the edges of the quilt.

Off-Centered Spotlights

Fig. 217.

You may reach for the unexpected by having a focus of light generally in the center of the quilt, but place that focus off-center, toward one corner. The lightest values will still be surrounded by mediums, but not in an evenly concentric fashion. Likewise, the darks will fill in the outer area in an uneven surrounding of the lights and mediums (Fig. 217).

Diagonal Movement of Light to Dark

Fig. 218.

Perhaps the spotlight is highlighting one corner of your quilt: as the eye moves from that corner to the opposing one, the values gradually grow darker (Fig. 218).

Reversals

Take each of the previous color strategies and consider the reverse placement of darks and lights, as diagrammed below.

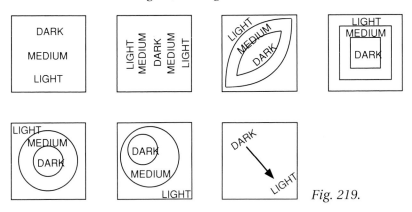

Fig. 219.

Multiples

More than one color strategy may be used in a quilt. Begin by picking out a shape or motif in your quilt design; change the fabric content (value) of that shape according to one of the color strategies as you proceed from one edge of the quilt to the other (below left).

Then apply a different color strategy to another shape (or grouping of shapes), or use it to fill in the entire background behind the original chosen shape (below right).

From combinations of color strategies comes true adventure in quiltmaking. You cannot predict what the eventual quilt will look like until you're ready to sew the final piece into place!

Creating the Third Dimension with Value

A tried-and-true principle of color value is that light values seem to advance toward the viewer from the flat surface, and dark values seem to recede into the background, even to go "behind" the flat surface of an art piece. That principle has been put to use in a number of quilts pictured in this book: in the flying geese ribbon surrounding the center blocks in San Diego Friends I (page 109); in the corners of Springtime Memories I (page 86); in Block Party Trees (page 83), where the boxes seem even more three-dimensional because of the dark values used in the "compartments" behind the tree blocks.

LIGHTS COMING FROM SINGULAR DIRECTIONS. When a beam of light shines on a three-dimensional object, each side is more or less brightly lit, depending on its position relative to the source of light. This principle was applied in the Barbara McCroskey Friendship Quilt by alternating lighter and darker values in the folded ribbon between blocks (page 82).

TRANSPARENCY. Any place in a design where one shape seems to cross another shape is an opportunity to use the principle of transparency. Make one shape very light, one shape very dark; where they cross, try to find the value which is right in between the light and the dark. Since we are not privileged to be able to mix paints to attain exact medium values, we come as close as we can with the fabrics available, and the mind's eye of the viewer completes the illusion.

In The Hales Quilt (page 113), note that the very light value which seemed to emanate from the corner blocks became a medium value where it crossed the dark "pedestals" supporting the north, south, east, and west blocks.

THREE-DIMENSIONAL MOTIFS. By using light, medium, and dark values in a consistent manner, one can make certain motifs "pop out" of the quilt surface. The flying geese border creating the central medallion of A Quilt of Kentucky Friendship (page 101) appears to be three-dimensional because of the alternating light and dark triangles marching around the central block. In Ice of Iris (page 106), the quadrilateral shapes in pink and purple seem to stand out from the gray background because of the consistent placement of light, medium, and dark values (even though their relative positions change from row to row).

Any time you have a four-sided figure in the design of your quilt, you have the option of creating the illusion that the viewer is looking down on a pyramid. The shape of the four-sided figure is immaterial; the key to this illusion is bisecting the figure corner to corner, both ways.

Fig. 220.

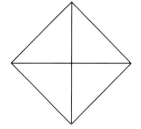
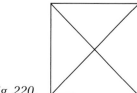
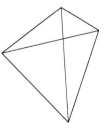

The success of the illusion depends on your careful attention to relative values in your fabrics. You need not only lights and darks, but also light mediums and dark mediums. Using only medium mediums will not be as effective (Fig. 221). Place the lights opposite the darks, and the light mediums and dark mediums always in the same position with respect to each other. In other words, think about the source of the light that is striking this pyramid, and carry that illusion throughout the quilt. If you establish one value arrangement, such as one of those you see in Figure 222, be consistent with that arrangement; don't change to the value arrangements on the right in other areas of the quilt.

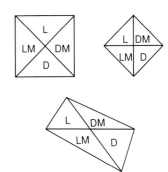

Fig. 221.

Richness of Surface

Many of the quilts in this book have a much more complex look than the line drawing would indicate, the reason being that in many cases, a drawn template shape may be filled not with a single fabric but with a combination of fabrics meant to enrich the surface.

One way to reach for the unexpected is to create a surface that offers some new detail, some fresh aspect, every time the viewer looks at it.

Enriching the surface by using more fabrics rather than fewer is another way of camouflaging where one block stops and its neighbor begins, or camouflaging where the body of the quilt stops and the border begins. In addition, enriching the surface eliminates some of the agony of finding "just the right fabric" for a given area of the quilt. In Block Party Trees (page 83), for example, there was no muslin or ecru or off-white which worked well as a light background in the center of the quilt; but by checkerboarding that area, the problem was solved.

A number of piecing methods are presented in this section to give you some mechanisms for creating richness of surface in areas where you may have traditionally used only a single fabric.

Fig. 222.

Strip Piecing

This term refers to sewing strips of fabric together first, then cutting a template shape out of multiples of fabrics sewn together, instead of from a single fabric.

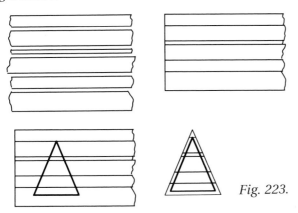

Fig. 223.

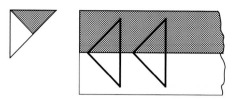

Fig. 224.

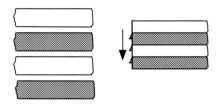

Fig. 225.

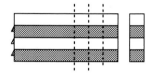

Fig. 226.

Strips of fabric are easily and quickly cut using a rotary cutter, cutting mat, and Plexiglas straightedge. Cut across the width of the fabric, and do not use longer than a half-width of fabric (about 22") for best results.

This technique can be used to create striped fabrics that help lead the eye from one area of the quilt to another, blend light and dark areas, or create texture in a piece that is too large in scale for a given area of quilt design.

Strip piecing can also be used to shorten piecing time. For instance, if you have two shapes that are going to be cut from the same fabrics throughout your quilt, you can sew the two fabrics together first, then cut the "double template" from the already assembled fabrics (Fig. 224).

Checkerboarding

Making checkerboarded fabric is strip piecing with one more step. To make a checkerboard, cut all strips the same width, ½" wider than the finished square in the checkerboard. Sew strips together with ¼" seams. Press all seams in one direction (Fig. 225). Cut these groupings of sewn strips perpendicular to the seams; cut to the same width the original strips were cut (Fig. 226). Sew these segments back together again, but invert every other segment to get the checkerboard effect. Since all the seams were pressed in the same direction, the seam allowances will now alternate direction and aid precision piecing.

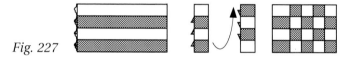

Fig. 227

Checkerboards can be made with dark and light strips alternated, or with numerous fabrics of many different values. You may also decide to cut the segments to varied widths, instead of only the width of the original strips, for some bold patterning in certain areas of your quilt.

Fig. 228.

I have often used checkerboards in the outermost border (see A Quilt of Kentucky Friendship, page 101) because there was not enough of a given fabric to complete the border. By checkerboarding, the fabric was "stretched" to meet the need.

Note the role the low-contrast checkerboard gridwork plays in the Barbara McCroskey Friendship Quilt (page 82). Without this subtle structure on which the ribbon of houses is stabilized, a much weaker design would have resulted.

Fan Strip Piecing

Another form of strip piecing uses segments of strips rather than half-widths of fabrics. Begin by sewing several strips 2" or wider to contrasting "separator strips," cut 1" wide (A). To sew these together, line up right sides together at an angle, instead of edges flush as in plain strip piecing. Sew ¼" seam along separator strip edge (B). Trim away triangle from lower strip (C). Press out (D).

Place next strip at an angle; sew ¼" seam, trim triangle (E), press out (F). Take one of the trimmed triangles and sew to original strip edge with ¼" seam; press out (G).

Place template piece over fan-pieced fabric, trace (H), and cut (I).

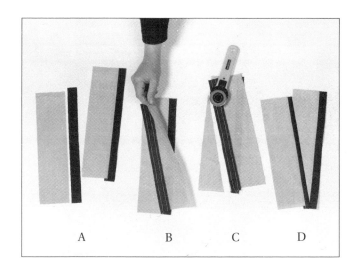

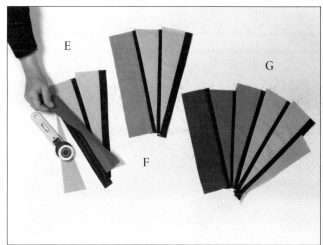

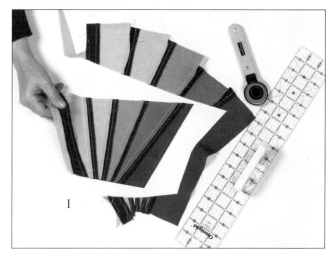

Darting

To add three-dimensional texture and interesting broken-striping patterns to your quilt surface, consider sewing darts into some of the strip-pieced fabrics. To begin, sew strips of varied widths together with ¼" seams. Fold perpendicular to the sewn seams, wrong sides together. Sew dart from right sides (A). Press out. Refold at an angle to existing dart. Sew another dart (B).

Fold at an angle on other side of original dart. Sew dart along this third fold (C). Press darts in one direction (D).

Place template, right side down, on wrong side of "darted fabric," trace (E) and cut out, adding seam allowance (F).

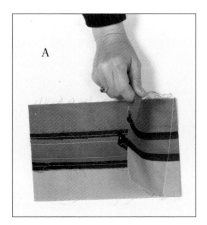

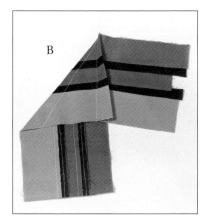

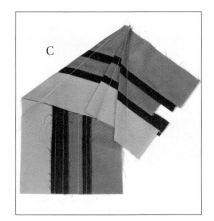

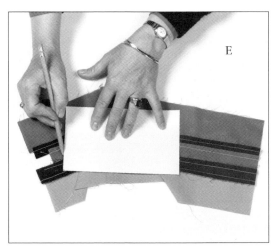

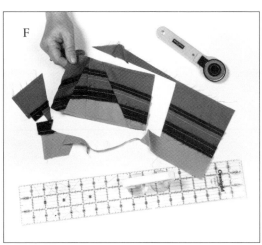

Putting It All Together: The Quilts

This chapter presents some of the quilts which appear in the color photos in this book, to give the reader a little more information on each of them. The sizes of the blocks and of the quilt in general are presented, and, where available, the stories behind the blocks and the quilts are told.

Even though this is not a pattern book, line drawings of the layouts of these quilts appear here to give the reader a better understanding of how the design devices presented in this book might be combined in real quilts. The individual quilt blocks within the quilts are represented as blank squares in most cases.

In the line drawings that follow, the solid lines are design lines; the dotted lines are seam lines that must be present in order to assemble these quilt tops. Techniques for richness of surface (such as checkerboarding or fan strip piecing—see pages 127–130) have been used in some of these quilts, and these details may or may not be sketched into the line drawings.

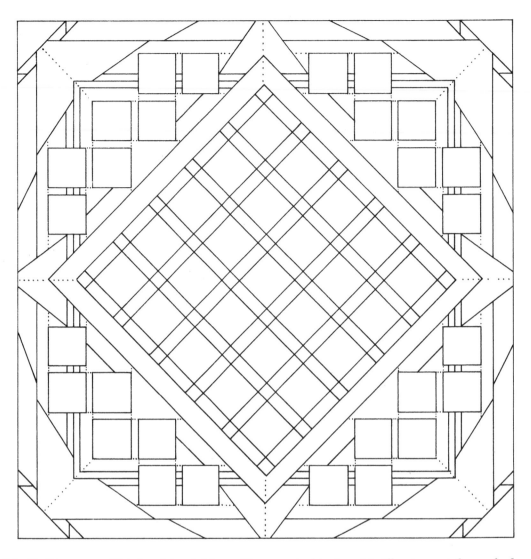

Ann Albertson's Friendship Quilt
Color photo on page 90

Owner: Ann M. Albertson,
    Escondido, California
Maker: Margaret J. Miller, San
    Marcos, California
Year Made: 1984
Size: 77" x 77"
The Blocks: Assorted sampler
patterns, all 6" squares

This is a friendship quilt presented to Ann M. Albertson at the end of her year as president of the Friendship Quilters Guild of Poway, a group she started in 1980 by putting an ad in the local newsprint advertiser distributed door-to-door in her community. She was one of the guiding lights of the early quilting community in the San Diego area. This quilt was made to commemorate not only her service to the guild, but the work she did in educating many sectors of the community in the world of quiltmaking.

The quilt was made as a surprise for Ann; the blocks were solicited in February on the theme of baskets and stars, two recurrent motifs in Ann's work. The topic for the May meeting, Ann's final guild meeting as president, was friendship quilts. Members were encouraged to bring friendship quilts for the show-and-tell section of the meeting. Ann brought a quilt of patriotic red, white, and blue that had been made in the mid-1970s (when so many bicentennial quilts in this same color scheme emerged and started the current resurgence of interest in quiltmaking). The quilt had been made by Ann's special quilting friends in Virginia, where she was living at the time; it was presented to her as a going-away gift before her move to San Diego.

What she didn't know was that we had written to those very quilting friends, and they too had sent blocks for the friendship quilt she would receive later on in the meeting.

These blocks total half the blocks submitted in a spring Basket block contest sponsored by The Quilt Shop in Stanwood, Washington, in early spring 1988. Mary Hales, the owner of the shop, assembled half of the blocks in a traditional manner, I assembled these, and everyone who had made a block for the contest had a chance to win one of the quilt tops.

The challenge of designing this quilt was first of all working in such light pinks—a new experience for me. The design emphasis became to stress the new angles which lead from the center blocks to the corners of the quilt and the blue diamond which appears to be behind all of the blocks. Those angles very unlike the 90° and 45° angles in the blocks seem to extend the lyrical and gentle quality of the baskets themselves.

The corner blocks were worked out on graph paper as the quilt layout was designed, and the flying geese reaching from the center to the corners help relate the corner blocks to the center grouping.

Working with light, medium, and dark values was an important factor in creating the illusion there are white lights emanating from the corner blocks toward the center of the quilt, crossing over the dark pink "pedestals" that seem to support the north, south, east, and west Basket blocks.

The Hales Quilt
Color photo on page 113

Owner/Quilter : Betty Charette, Aberdeen, Washington
Maker: Margaret J. Miller, Woodinville, Washington
Year Made: 1988
Size: 61" x 61"
The Blocks: Assorted basket patterns, all 12" blocks

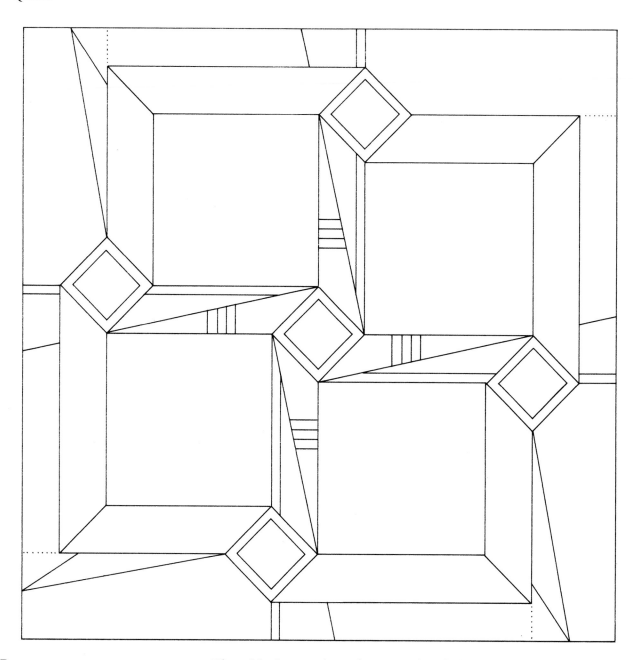

Fiesta Rose
Color photo on page 94

Owner/Maker: Susan M. Connoley,
  Gig Harbor, Washington
Year Made: 1990
Size: 66" x 66"
The Blocks: The four 19" blocks
were started in a class; two of the
patterns came possibly from
Quilter's Newsletter, the others were
original designs. The five 8" blocks
were salvaged from a quilt top, the
center of which was chewed up by
the family dog.

These blocks were brought to my class "Old Blocks to New Quilts," a
three-session class in which students could try some innovative ways of
creating quilt tops with blocks they had collected. Imagine the shock
waves that went over the class when Sue brought this quilt as a top—
already sewn together—at the beginning of the second session.

Part of Sue's challenge to herself was to take a predictable comple-
mentary color scheme (red and green) and introduce every other color
into the quilt top—which she did. She also was pleased with the sense
of spontaneity given by the "confetti" appliqué pieces sprinkled over
the quilt.

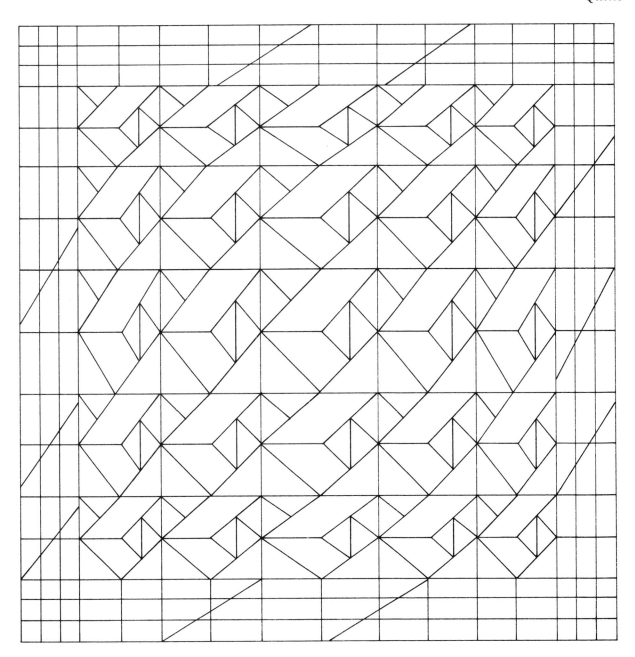

Though a single pattern was used throughout the body of this quilt, the block appears in the form of squares, horizontal rectangles, and vertical rectangles.

This is part of my Bloomin' Quilt Grids series of quilts, three of which are made of this identical pattern block. In this series, the combination of squares and horizontal and vertical rectangles creates the illusion of a domelike image in the center of the quilt, or at least of curves where there are no curved seams.

In this particular piece, the curves are not so obvious within the body of the work, so the slanted seams that divide the two color schemes in the checkerboard border help preserve whatever curves are evident in the quilt's center.

Bloomin' Quilt Grids has proven for me to be a very versatile graphic mechanism for experimenting with the movement of color. This will be my subject in an upcoming book.

Sea Route
Color photo on page 117

Owner/Maker: Margaret J. Miller, Woodinville, Washington
Year Made: 1986
Size: 59" x 59"
The Blocks: This untitled block was designed by Michael James of Massachusetts and distributed to his students in a class on color in contemporary quilts. Quite a number of quilts based on this block have been made by Mr. James's students, and he granted permission for this quilt's inclusion in this book.

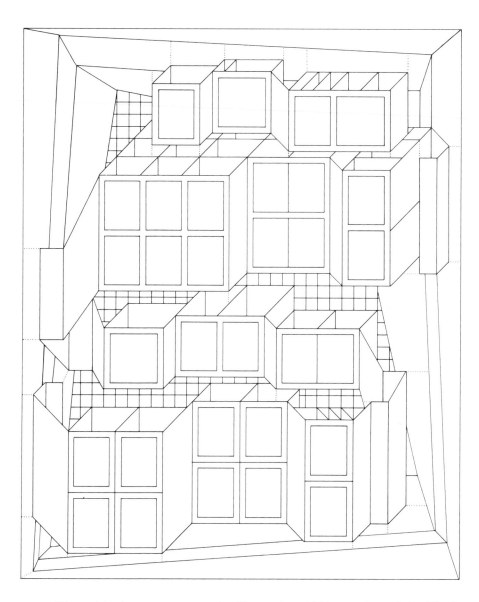

Block Party Trees
Color photo on page 83

Owner/Maker: Margaret J. Miller,
   Woodinville, Washington
Year Made: 1990
Size: 74" x 90"
The Blocks: 6" x 8" and 8" x 8". This
block is The Alpine Tree pattern
from Carolann Palmer's book
Branching Out—Tree Quilts (published by That Patchwork Place).
The original block was an 8" square;
by shaving an inch or two off the
side edges, I transformed most of
the blocks into rectangles, and the
quilt then became an experiment in
how many ways the rectangles
could be assembled into boxlike
units.

These blocks were won at the November 1989 meeting of the Block
Party Quilters guild of Kirkland, Washington. Every month this guild
prints the pattern for a "charm quilt" block in the newsletter. For each
block submitted, the maker's name goes into a hat for a chance to win
an entire group of blocks. This block was so easy to make, and it was such
fun to vary the trees with checkerboards and slashed insertions, I submitted twenty-two blocks, and won a set of twenty-eight blocks . . . and
ended up making three more singles to finish out the top row of the quilt.

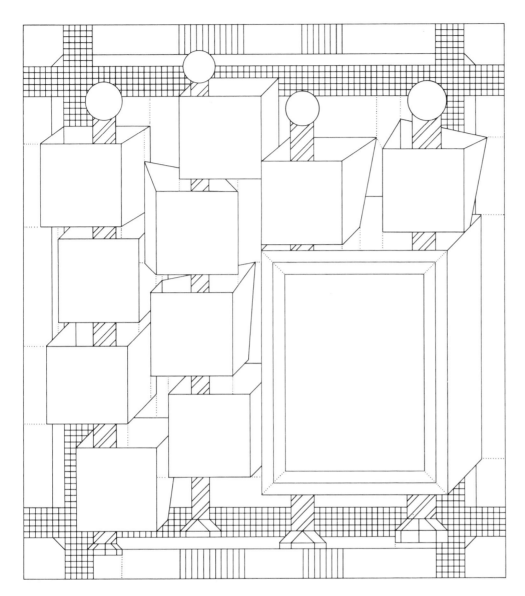

These blocks were made by some of Rachel's quilting friends early in her quiltmaking career—Rachel herself had appliquéd the large rectangular block. The blocks had lain in a shopping bag for years, covered by a number of flowered fabrics Rachel was collecting to assemble the quilt top. On a visit to Rachel's in 1988, during a discussion of old sampler blocks one might never put together, I came into possession of the blocks and the flowery fabrics.

My inspiration for putting these blocks together was Rachel herself. Rachel is the kind of friend with such a charmingly flamboyant style and keen sense of humor that when you see her coming toward you, you begin to giggle—because you know she will probably say something funny right off the bat . . . and thus the theme for her sampler blocks became open boxes of a happily distorted shape, strung on barber poles.

To my way of thinking, the soft Victorian-posy fabrics Rachel had assembled didn't seem to go either with the crayon-color blocks or with my impression of their owner; however, I did manage to use some of them (the print of pink flowers on a white background in the outer border was one of those fabrics). The reason there is vertical striping in the top and bottom borders is that I ran out of that pink posy fabric.

Rachel Kincy Clark's Friendship Quilt
Color photo on page 96

Owner: Rachel Kincy Clark, Watsonville, California
Maker: Margaret J. Miller, San Marcos, California
Year Made: 1989
Size: 83" x 93"
The Blocks: Assorted pieced and appliqué blocks, Pennsylvania Dutch motif, primary colors. Ten 14" blocks, one 32" x 41" block.

**Gathering Basket: A Signature
Quilt**
Color photo on page 60

Owner/Maker: Cody M. Mazuran,
Salt Lake City, Utah
Year Made: 1989
Size: 53" x 54"
The Blocks: Signature strips, 1½"
wide; assorted sampler blocks, 6",
7", or 8" square (without borders)

The names on this quilt were gathered by Cody Mazuran from the women in her church group. The following are her words, written in early May 1990:

The blocks I chose to incorporate in the design were not only charming in their own right but significant when I thought about my friends.

Flower Garden: Bloom where you are planted.
Evening Star: Working late into the night planning and stitching that quilt.
Triple Rail Fence: Fence those kids in but give them an ample gate.
Devil's Puzzle: Something we spent a lot of time trying to figure out.
Dresden Plate: Another something we spent a lot of time trying to figure out—just how to have food every time we met and still stay within the budget.
Grandmother's Fan: A fan was always in my grandmother's purse. I put a box of tissue in mine.
Log Cabin: America's favorite. Red square in the center—a warm hearth, yellow square, a light in the window.
House Block: A place where people can go to find peace, warmth, and love.
Gathering Basket: There is no end to what is in the Gathering Basket when its contents are shared with others.

After a year of poring over the resulting set of fifty friendship blocks, and completing more urgent projects (such as the writing of this book), it was time to begin working with these special blocks. The sudden desire to include them in this *Blockbuster Quilts* collection gave me the impetus to sit down and design the quilts which would house them.

Before I began to design, the blocks had to be measured and categorized as to size. Construction paper blanks were made of a size to include the block plus a 1" border around each. As I sat down to begin putting these blocks together, I thought that two quilts would result—but as work progressed, it became obvious that there would have to be three quilts to properly accommodate all those blocks (many of which were 12" square). All three quilts were drafted to scale on graph paper one Saturday morning—when the timing is right, the designs pour out.

In the grouping of fifty blocks, all but one block could be used as a square; the one block which had to be used as a diamond was included as the center of this quilt. A touching farewell gift was Pat Scoville's offer to quilt the quilt I would make from the farewell blocks . . . little did she know that they would be made into *three* quilts! She quilted this one; I will hand quilt the other two—and I take the time to hand quilt only the most special quilts now.

San Diego Friends I
Color photo on page 109

Owner/Maker: Margaret J. Miller, Woodinville, Washington
Quilters: Pat Scoville, Ann Albertson, Patty B. Smith, Jan Inouye, Judy Mathieson
Year Made: 1990
Size: 66" x 84"
The Blocks: Assorted sampler blocks, given to me as farewell friendship blocks when I moved from the San Diego area after living there ten years. Certain fabrics were purchased to guarantee a somewhat unified result. However, the following criteria went to the block makers along with those fabrics: "1) add as many fabrics or colors as you wish; 2) make either an 8", 10", or 12" block; 3) make the pattern of your choice or an original design."

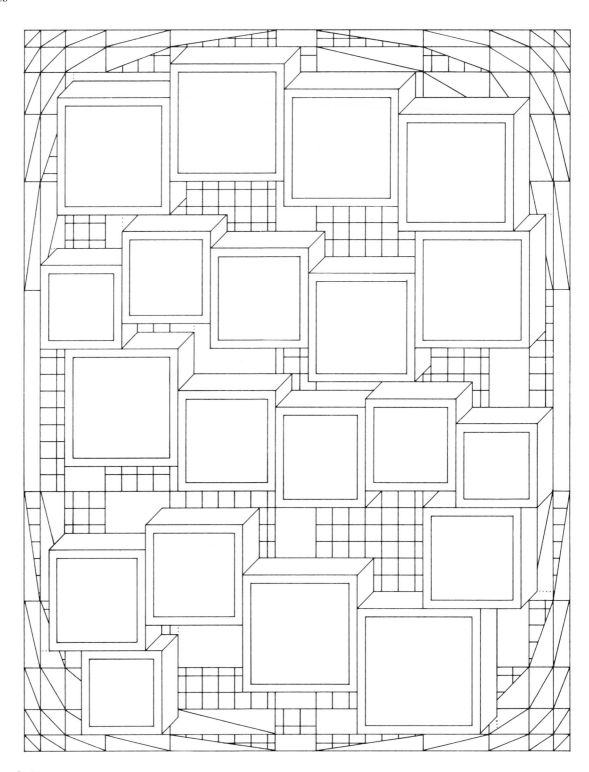

San Diego Friends II
Color photo on page 37

Owner/Maker: Margaret J. Miller,
  Woodinville, Washington
Year Made: 1990
Size: 65" x 84"
The Blocks: See notes under San
Diego Friends I, page 139.

I wanted to continue to explore a setting that presented a ribbon of blocks, similar to the Barbara McCroskey Friendship Quilt (page 82) but without the connecting ribbon. It was interesting how dimensional this arrangement became, even though there was not that much difference in size among the blocks used.

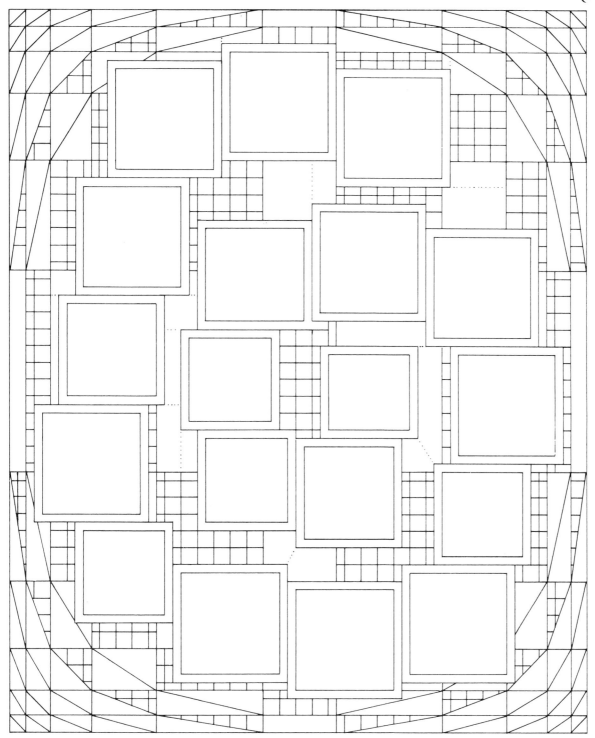

Since this would be the third quilt in a triptych whose center would be San Diego Friends I, I wanted to arrange the blocks in a ribbon as in San Diego Friends II, but in a different configuration.

At the time I was working on these designs, I had agreed to appliqué a Nautilus Shell block for a charity quilt; hence the idea arose to arrange the blocks in a spiral formation.

San Diego Friends III
Color photo on page 38

Owner/Maker: Margaret J. Miller, Woodinville, Washington
Year Made: 1990
Size: 71" x 84"
The Blocks: See notes under San Diego Friends I, page 139.

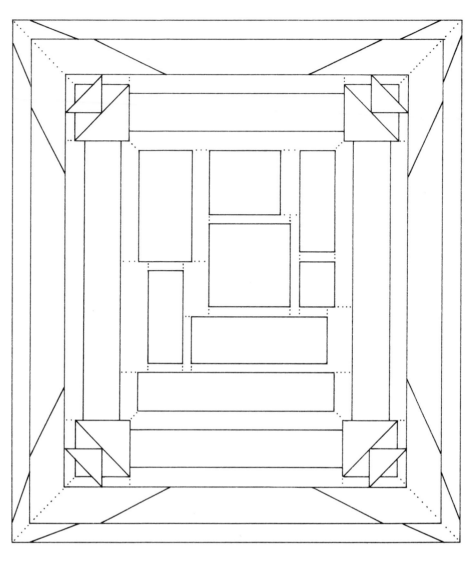

Friendship Quilters Guild Banner
Color photo on page 62

Owner: Friendship Quilters Guild, Poway, California

Maker: Blocks made by early members of Friendship Quilters Guild, top designed and assembled by Margaret J. Miller, quilting by members of Friendship Quilters Guild of Poway

Year Made: 1984

Size: 49" x 55"

The Blocks: The blocks are variously sized squares and rectangles, of motifs meaningful to the guild—sewing implements and tools, the state bird and flower of California, the Friendship Star block, and a schoolhouse with lights in the windows, as the guild meets evenings at a public school.

The blocks were made early in the history of the Friendship Quilters Guild of Poway by various members. This is one of the first groupings of disparate blocks I offered to put together for someone else. But it was a project I was honored to take on, since this is the group that sponsored the two-day Nancy Crow workshop in 1981 that served as a critical first step for me toward becoming the quiltmaker I am today. Nancy Crow has continued to be a strong influence on my work habits and my attitude toward myself as an artist, and I will be forever indebted to Friendship Quilters for facilitating that influence.

This quilt was a commission by *Quilting Today* magazine (Chitra Publications, New Milford, Pennsylvania). It was part of the launching of their new magazine *Traditional Quiltworks*. The quilt was to be on the cover of the premiere issue, and everyone who subscribed to the new magazine would have a chance to win it.

The two criteria for the commission were that the quilt be blue, and there had to be recognizable traditional quilt blocks in it. (This was stipulated because I was getting a reputation for distorting traditional blocks rather drastically at the time.)

Starry, Starry Sampler
Color photo on page 27

Owner: Jeanne Duncan, Bartlesville, Oklahoma
Maker: Margaret J. Miller, San Marcos, California
Year Made: 1988
Size: 64" x 64"
The Blocks: Rectangle—Keywest Beauty (8" x 12"); 9" Squares—
1. Wisconsin 2. Vermont 3. North Carolina Var. 4. California Var.
5. Vermont 6. California Var.
7. St. Paul Var. 8. Montana Var.
The blocks came from Barbara Bannister and Edna Paris Ford's patchwork pattern books *State Capitals Quilt Blocks* and *The United States Patchwork Pattern Book.*

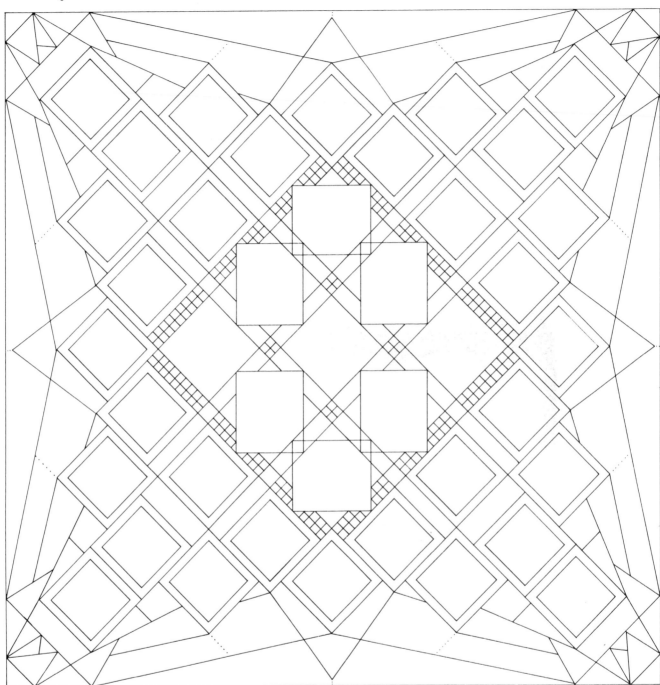

Bernice's Baskets
Color photo on page 36

Owner: Bernice McCoy Stone,
    Kensington, California
Maker: Margaret J. Miller,
    Woodinville, Washington
Year Made: 1990
Size: 83" x 83"
The Blocks: Assorted basket patterns.

Bernice brought all these blocks to my class "Reach for the Unexpected in Pieced Surface Design" at the Empty Spools Conference in Monterey, California, in the spring of 1989. The minute she put them up on the design wall, I fell in love with them and mentally relished the challenge of putting such a diverse group of blocks together into a meaningful pieced surface. Since Bernice had brought several bags of other blocks to work with in the class, I asked if I could take them and see what I could come up with. The resulting quilt top was presented to Bernice as a surprise at the Empty Spools Conference a year later in Monterey.

The blocks in this quilt (excluding the gray ones) constitute only half of a set of blocks-of-the-month won by Myrna Sablick when she lived in San Diego and was a member of the Canyon Quilters Guild. When she moved from San Diego, she donated this set of blocks to be made into a raffle quilt. I offered to set the blocks for the guild, as I had been the speaker at their first meeting.

The blocks were irregular in size, as they had been made by quite a number of people. I had to disassemble some of them in order to piece in the triangles which extend from the edge of one block into the interior of some of the neighboring blocks.

Amish Lights
Color photo on page 77

Owner: Canyon Quilters Guild, San Diego, California
Maker: Margaret J. Miller, Woodinville, Washington
Year Made: 1989
Size: 65" x 87"
The Blocks: 9" Churn Dash, Amish-type color scheme

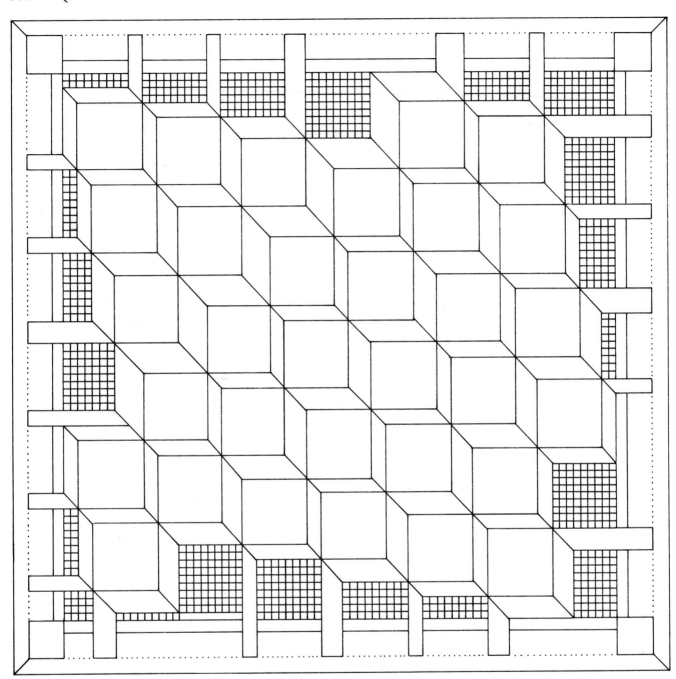

Martha Williams Friendship Quilt
Color photo on page 80

Owner: Martha Williams, Kent, Washington
Maker: Margaret J. Miller, San Marcos, California
Year Made: 1986
Size: 92" x 88"
The Blocks: Assorted 9" sampler blocks, given to Martha unset in thanks for her term of service as president of Evergreen Piecemakers (Kent, Washington)

Martha was the first person to invite me not only out-of-state to teach, but to teach for a multi-day workshop. The three-day "Quilter's Slumber Party," as she called it, was held in her home. Attendees came in recreational vehicles with sleeping bags under their arms. During the course of the workshop, talk of this set of quilt blocks surfaced, and it was evident that Martha had not had a chance to put them together (and no committee had emerged to do so, either).

With great inner trepidation, I offered to set the blocks together for Martha, to thank her for having me teach: a kind of hostess gift. Besides, I knew she was about to leave the country to work for two years as a social worker in Malaysia. I would have plenty of time to work on them. . . .

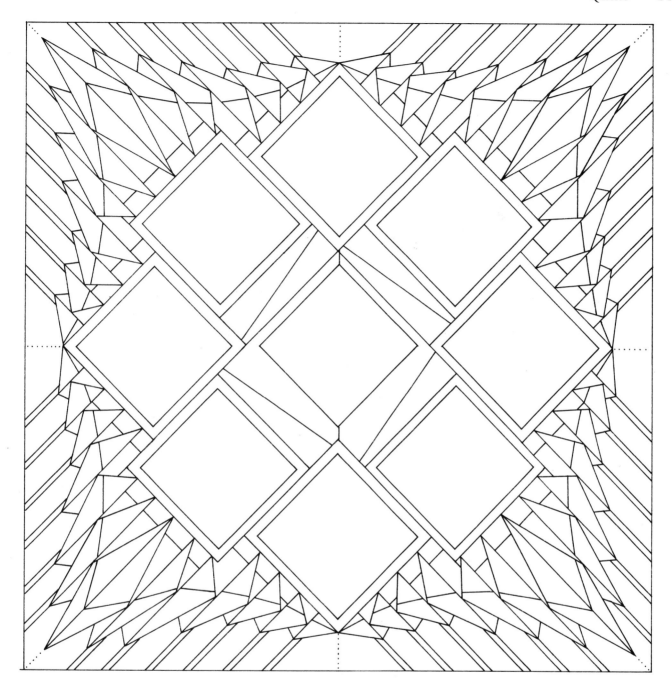

The goal of this quilt was to preserve the gentle nature of the blocks, yet work further with the flying geese motif in the border. This quilt reaches for the unexpected a bit more, perhaps, than does Springtime Memories I, even though there are many similarities between the two.

Notice the frame around the central block. In the quilt Springtime Memories I, the division is a seam line parallel to the edges of the block. In Springtime Memories II, that line was purposely slanted.

This quilt is a good illustration of my emerging motto, "Never use two fabrics where you can use twenty." Note the use of multiple fabrics between the inner flying geese triangles. The pale border beyond the pieced green triangles is strip pieced to add richness of surface.

Springtime Memories II
Color photo on page 59

Owner: Evelyn M. Griffin, Puyallup, Washington
Maker: Margaret J. Miller, Woodinville, Washington
Year Made: 1990
Size: 68" x 68"
The Blocks: Nine 12" blocks—the rest of the set from the "Springtime Memories" block contest at The Quilt Barn, Puyallup, Washington (Evelyn M. Griffin, owner)

Allen's Teenage Quilt
Color photo on page 58

Owner: Allen Edward Miller
Maker: Margaret J. Miller (Allen's
    mother), San Marcos, California
Year Made: 1988
Size: 54" x 93"
The Blocks: appliqué maple leaf,
airplanes, frogs, and various stars

A few years ago I visited Joan Schulze, a maker of art quilts from San Jose, California, and mother of four. She told me about teenage quilts—which ideally are made by the mother and child and include motifs significant to the child and the family. The quilt is presented to the child on his/her twelfth birthday, so that no matter how estranged the parents and child may become during the turbulent teenage years, the love of the parents goes over the child every night—whether he/she wants it or not! I set out, then, to make teenage quilts for my own sons—then ages eleven and thirteen.

Allen wanted only the American flag and the Canadian flag on his teenage quilt, since we adopted him in Canada as an infant, and he became a U.S. citizen at age thirteen. Though I will probably make him that quilt someday, I couldn't bring myself to do such a plain one for his first teenage quilt.

So the red and white maple leaf blocks represent the Canadian flag; the blue/white stars and red/white strips represent the United States flag. The four frog blocks in the corners represent Allen's fascination with anything in nature that moves; they remind me of the many hours he spent in the fields around our home in southern California, catching insects, worms, frogs, snakes, and assorted creatures. The airplane blocks symbolize his longstanding determination to be a flyer someday.

Assembling the blocks into this quilt top was my present to Pat on her fortieth birthday. The blocks are from her quilting friends in Kentucky, where she lived for five years (and owned a quilt shop for part of that time). Since I had met many of the quiltmakers who had made these friendship blocks as a going-away present for Pat, working with them was like revisiting old friends, and the whole project was a delight.

This quilt was published in the Quilt Art '89 Engagement Calendar by the American Quilters Society. Pat hand quilted this piece herself, and added a lot of magic to it by incorporating curving lines over the dark green areas.

A Quilt of Kentucky Friendship
Color photo on page 101

Owner: Pat Scoville, Westlake Village, California
Maker: Margaret J. Miller, San Marcos, California
Quilter: Pat Scoville, Westlake Village, California
Year Made: 1988
Size: 101" x 114"
The Blocks: Assorted sampler blocks. The center block, Waveland Revisited, is 22" square; two corner blocks 12" square; twenty-five 10" blocks. All made by Pat Scoville's quilting friends in the Kentucky Heritage Quilting Society.

Thompson Retirement Quilt
Color photo on page 97

Owner: Dr. and Mrs. Arthur H.
    Thompson, College Park,
    Maryland
Maker: Margaret J. Miller,
    San Marcos, California;
    blocks by children of Dr. and
    Mrs. Thompson
Year Made: 1983
Size: 52" x 52"
The Blocks: Four 14" blocks drawn
with liquid embroidery pens

The blocks are drawings depicting things and events special to our family. They were done by my sister, two brothers, and myself as a tribute to our father on the occasion of his retirement from thirty years of being on the University of Maryland faculty.

The colors were chosen to reflect his life's work, research in pomology (the science of pome fruits). Much of his work was done in apple orchards, so the color choices were meant to evoke earth, trees, leaves, apples, and sunshine. Extra red was added because Dad is known for his love of this color—he once had one office wall painted red, and his red socks are legendary.

These blocks are part of the group resulting from the "Springtime Memories" block contest sponsored by The Quilt Barn in Puyallup, Washington. Two sizes of blocks were solicited, but only 12" blocks were entered. In order to make a more interesting surface, one fan block was easily disassembled to be used as four 6" blocks without destroying the blocks' integrity in the total quilt.

The light values that continued almost to the corners of the quilt were used to extend the X feeling formed by the central blocks. The altered angle represented by the darkest purple fabric was purposely done to give relief from the preponderance of 45° and 90° angles in the quilt.

Springtime Memories I
Color photo on page 86

Owner: Evelyn M. Griffin, Puyallup, Washington
Maker: Margaret J. Miller, Woodinville, Washington
Year Made: 1990
Size: 55" x 55"
The Blocks: Six 12" blocks; one of these was disassembled to create four 6" blocks.

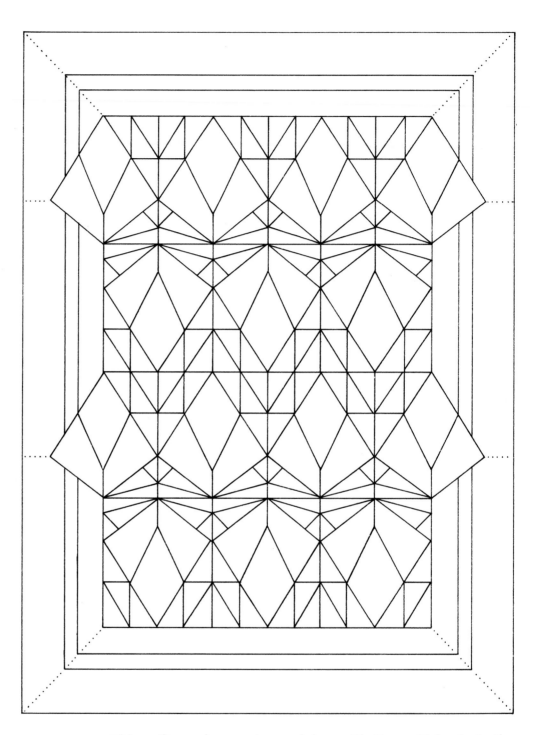

Ice of Iris
Color photo on page 106

Owner: Marjory R. Crist, Santa
  Rosa, California
Maker: Margaret J. Miller,
  San Marcos, California
Year Made: 1984
Size: 36" x 47"
The Blocks: 7¾" x 8½" rectangular
adaptations of the traditional Hen
and Chicks block

This quilt was begun at a workshop with Nancy Halperin in the shadow of the Golden Gate Bridge at Pt. Bonita, California. The workshop was on dyeing and painting techniques for fabrics to be used in a quilt project. I got very confused, however, over the numerous types of dyeing we were attempting, and never did use in this project any of the hand-processed fabrics from that week.

One of my favorite quilts is an early one by Nancy Halperin on the theme of crocuses, and I am sure it was on my mind as this piece emerged that January week at Pt. Bonita.

This quilt resulted from my class "Old Blocks to New Quilts," three sessions on creating innovative settings for traditional quilt blocks.

United Against All Odds
Color photo on page 115

Owner/Maker: Sara Quattlebaum, Olympia, Washington
Year Made: 1990
Size: 84" x 84"
The Blocks: Assorted sampler blocks

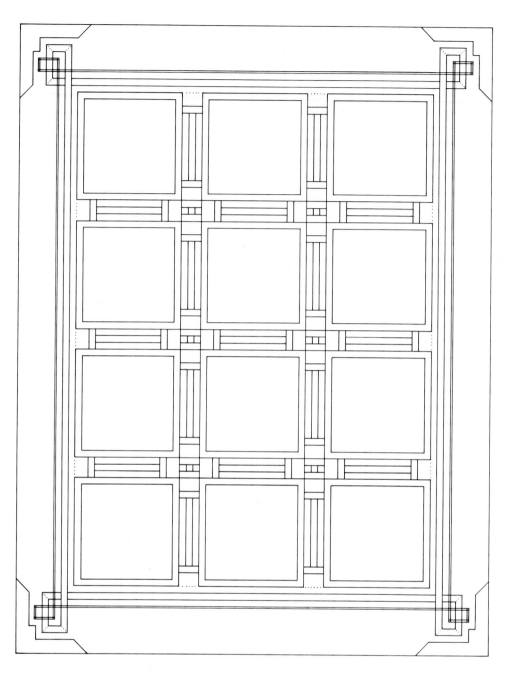

Poppy II
Color photo on page 76

Owner/Maker: Margaret J. Miller,
  San Marcos, California
Year Made: 1980
Size: 72" x 93"
The Blocks: The stained glass appliqué
pattern used in these 12" blocks was
one I designed and sold in the early
1980s as part of my pattern business,
Tanglethread Junction.

The blocks in this quilt took so long to do, because of the amount of
handwork involved, that I started embroidering the date the block was
finished into each one. As the deadline for finishing the quilt drew
nearer, the dates grew closer together in time—there are three blocks
which have the same finishing date on them!

The design of the setting for these blocks was carefully done to
enhance the strong design within the blocks, yet contain it effectively at
the same time. The pieced sashing strips and setting squares carry out
the floral theme in a geometric fashion.

The two black stripes that surround the grouping of blocks were
appliquéd on. Unfortunately, there was an irregular tear across one
corner of the quilt top, and no more rust fabric to replace any segment
of the border. Hence the black "photo corners" were appliquéd over the
corners of the quilt. This is yet another example of design disasters
turning into design delights.

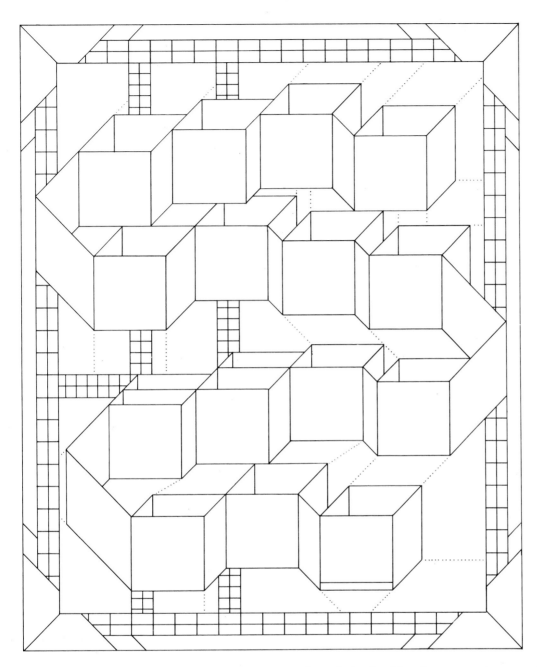

These blocks were made for Barbara by her friends in the Monday Night Quilting Group, in which she quilted for years in Poway, California. When she moved from Poway to Indiana, these blocks in the form of this quilt top went with her.

The design adventure of this quilt was making the house blocks appear to be the fronts of moving boxes, strung on a cardboard ribbon that snaked its way up the quilt. Special attention was paid to color in that the cardboard "ribbon" is a lighter value when it angles one direction than when it turns the opposite direction. Also, notice that the ribbon goes out into the border in two different places at the sides of the quilt, thus helping camouflage where the blocks stop and the border begins.

The role of the low-contrast checkerboard in the background behind the ribbon of boxes is a crucial one; the checkerboard forms a kind of gridwork on which to "hang" the ribbon of houses.

Barbara McCroskey Friendship Quilt
Color photo on page 82

Owner: Barbara McCroskey, Carmel, Indiana
Maker: Margaret J. Miller, San Marcos, California
Year Made: 1987
Size: 70" x 83"
The Blocks: House on the Hill blocks, all 10" squares

Loma's Dutch Girls
Color photo on page 73

Owner: Loma Gene Miller Hersom, San Jose, California

Maker: Margaret J. Miller (Loma's niece by marriage), San Marcos, California

Makers of the Blocks: Mrs. M. Allen Miller (mother of the present owner) and Mrs. Ben Wilson, Pecos, Texas

Year Made: 1988 (blocks probably made in 1930s)

Size: 62" x 98"

The Blocks: Dutch Girl Blocks, 11" x 13" rectangles; border blocks, 9" squares; pattern is a variation of Little Rock block

These blocks are only half of a group made in Texas in the 1930s. The following is what Loma G. Hersom wrote about them in April 1990: "In the early 1930s, there were twenty-four 'Dutch Girl' quilt blocks made to be equally divided between my sister, Minnie Lea Miller Lafferty, and me. It is unknown if the blocks were made by one person or by my mother, Myrtle Miller, and Mrs. Wilson, a longtime family friend. It was several years after mother died that Lea and I divided the blocks by taking turns in selecting a block."

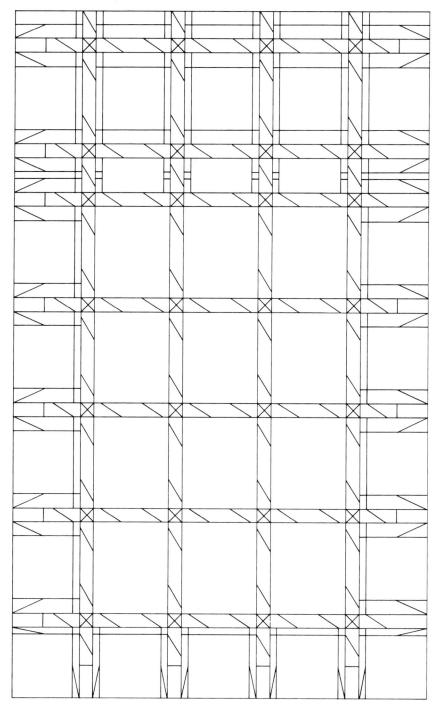

I learned about teenage quilts (see explanation under Allen's Teenage Quilt, page 148) too late for David and me to design his teenage quilt together, so I did the next best thing: used blocks he had designed as a child as the basis for his teenage quilt. The origin of the maple leaf block is unknown; it appears in what was a blank space in the blocks David drew. It is included because he was born in the fall. The separation between the central body of blocks and the outer row was going to be filled with those hand-pieced 5" maple leaves, but I ran out of time, and substituted strip-pieced darting (see page 130) in order to have the top assembled for his birthday. In retrospect, this was a better design choice than fifty-three more hand-pieced leaves to fill this area.

David's Teenage Quilt
Color photo on page 18

Owner: David Andrew Miller
Maker: Margaret J. Miller (David's mother), San Marcos, California
Year Made: 1985
Size: 72" x 98"
The Blocks: The two blocks which make up this quilt (they are checkerboarded in the center, and one of them forms the border) were drawn on graph paper by David at age eight or nine. He, like children of other quiltmakers, liked to play with graph paper and colored pencils when I was working on graph paper designing my early quilts. The maple leaf blocks are 5½" square, hand pieced, and the only part of the block not designed by David (though the source of this block is now unknown).

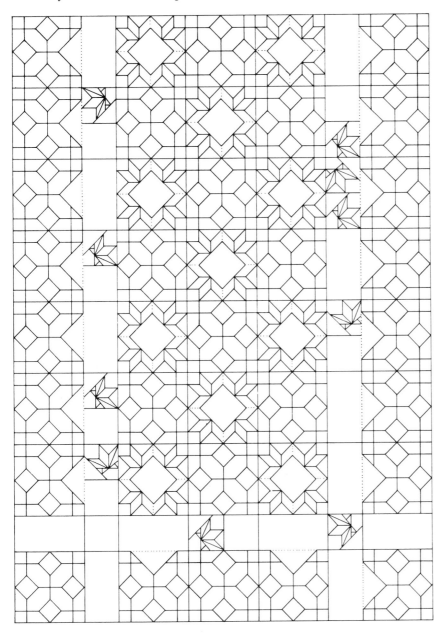

<u>A</u>ppendix A

Graph Paper to Templates: Hints on Template Making

The method explained below for making templates is the method I use in quiltmaking. It involves cutting out templates whose edge is the stitching line: I do not add a seam allowance before the template is cut out, a procedure that is normally used for hand piecing.

The reason this method is especially useful for making the types of quilts described in this book, is that once you give yourself permission to use very elongated or otherwise odd shapes in your patchwork, you often need an actual stitching line drawn on your fabric. To use Template-Free™ techniques or to make a template with seam allowance already included for piecing would make machine piecing of these designs too awkward.

Making Templates

Tools and Supplies

Drawing of block (or entire quilt surface) to scale, with templates labeled with a letter or number

Graph paper (eight or ten squares to the inch, cross-section pad—heavier blue line appears every inch—11" x 17" or 17" x 22"). Whichever scale of graph paper you choose, stick with it—don't change mid-project.

Long ruler

Sharp pencil

Eraser

Rotary cutting tool (used only for paper—so you don't dull the rotary cutter you use for fabric)

Plexiglas straightedge

Rotary cutting surface

Spray adhesive

Rubber cement

Scotch tape

Posterboard from drugstore or dime store

Procedure

On your scale drawing, assign a letter to each shape that will need to be cut as a template. Draw block (or portion of quilt) full size from your scale drawing as shown at the top of page 159.

Note: If you are drawing a section of the quilt which is larger than your graph paper, join a second sheet by first cutting off the corners of the sheet to be added. Thus, you will be able to line up both horizontal and vertical lines at the same time on your graph paper.

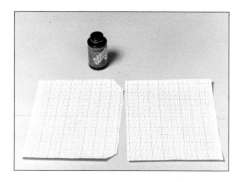

Scale: 1 small square on graph paper equals 1 square inch, life size.

Line up the two sheets of paper; apply rubber cement where the two sheets overlap. Adhere one paper to the other, checking to see that all graph-paper lines are lined up precisely. To join posterboard, line up edges flush, put Scotch tape over both sides of the seam—top and underside—for a stronger joining. Spray a sheet of posterboard with adhesive. Attach your graph-paper drawing by rolling it onto the posterboard, pressing out all bubbles with your forearm as you go, thus:

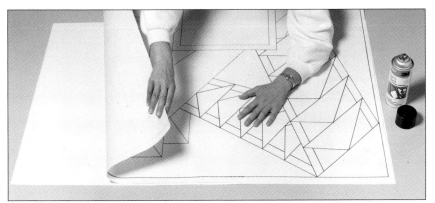

Transfer template letters from your scale drawing to full-size templates. Draw in grain lines if you want to be sure that the straight (lengthwise) grain is on a particular edge. Indicate it with a long arrow, as shown in the figure to the right.

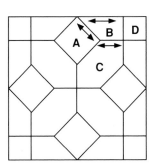

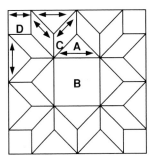

Now you are ready to cut out the individual templates with your rotary cutter and Plexiglas straightedge.

If I am making a very complex quilt, I will leave the full-size posterboard drafting of the block intact until I am ready to cut a particular template from that block out of fabric.

If the quilt is very large, or is one with many shapes repeated in it, you do not have to draw out the entire quilt full size. I draw only a portion of the quilt at a time, as I need the template pieces.

If you have some template pieces to draft that are larger than your rulers, you may use two yardsticks. (This method was used in the Block Party Trees quilt, page 83. In that quilt, a long, narrow triangle extends the entire width of the quilt top.)

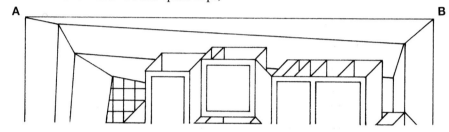

On your scale drawing, count the number of small squares along the top edge of the quilt (line AB). (In Block Party Trees, the top edge was seventy-four squares long.) Draw a line along one of the heavier blue lines on your graph paper 74" long. (You will need to join a number of pieces of graph paper before drawing this line.)

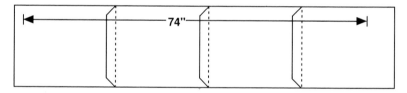

Point C on the scale drawing is four little squares down and five little squares to the left of point B. So, on your full-size drawing, count down 4" and move 5" to the left to mark point C. Join points B and C with a line.

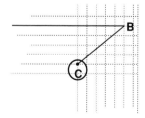

Point D on the scale drawing is one little square down and six little squares to the right of point A. So, on your full-size drawing, count down 1" and move 6" to the right to mark point D. Join points A and D with a straight line.

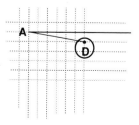

To connect points C and D, which obviously is a line longer than any ruler you have, take two yardsticks and line them up end to end, and hold a Plexiglas ruler next to them so they form a straight line, thus:

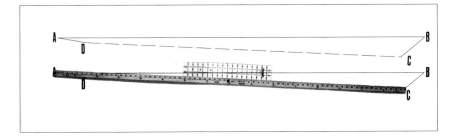

By rotating this new "ruler" so it touches both points C and D, you can draw the final edge of the template in question. Another method for drawing a line longer than a standard yardstick: first, hold two yardsticks together side by side, overlapping their ends as in the photo below.

In order to join points C and D, make the north side of one yardstick touch point C, and the south side of the other yardstick touch point D.

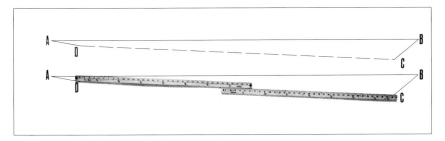

You may then draw partial lines from points A and B to where the yardsticks join. Remove yardsticks. Place ruler between given lines; complete template line.

Keeping Organized

When you have separate templates for every block, you may want to make a file folder for each block. This way, every time you use a template, you will return it to that folder for easy retrieval as needed. I use a vertical office file to hold my folders of templates.

Appendix B
Guide to Block Patterns Used in This Book

Most of the blocks used in this book were found in source books of patchwork patterns (see Bibliography for a complete listing). Below are the blocks and their pattern names as they appeared in these sources. It is possible the same blocks appear in other sources under different names.

The blocks are listed in the order in which they first appeared in this book. Many of them were used more than once.

Below each pattern is the block name, the source book, and page number, where known; and the page numbers of this book where the block is used in design exercises.

The codes indicating the source book are as follows:

BB	Barbara Brackman, *An Encyclopedia of Pieced Quilt Patterns*
JB	Jinny Beyer, *The Quilter's Album of Blocks & Borders*
SL4P	Shirley Liby, *Exploring Four Patch*
JM	Judy Martin, *Judy Martin's Ultimate Book of Quilt Block Patterns*
CP	Carolann Palmer, *Branching Out—Tree Quilts*

Block Sketch, Name, & Source

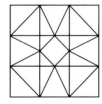

Doris's Delight
BB #1626, p. 209
Found in this book,
on pages 12, 50, 51

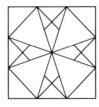

A Variation of Vermont
BB #2739, p. 373
Found in this book,
on page 12

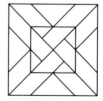

Whirligig I
JB, p. 47 (designed by Marcia
Aasmundstad, 1980)
Found in this book,
on pages 13, 15, 17, 20, 21, 24,
26, 29, 34, 35, 39, 41, 42, 54, 57

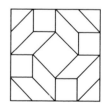

Bachelor's Puzzle
JB, p. 44
Found in this book,
on pages 14, 15, 20, 21,
24, 29, 35, 39, 41, 42

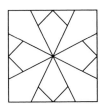

Variation of Key West Star
BB #2719, p. 371
Found in this book,
on pages 13, 15, 20–24, 26,
29, 32–34, 55, 56

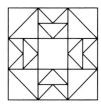

Capital T
JB, p. 73
Found in this book,
on pages 15, 17, 22, 24, 29,
31–33, 39, 41, 42

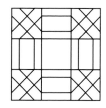

Tangled Garter
JB, p. 72
Found in this book,
on page 15

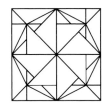

Lucky Star
BB #1301, p. 155
Found in this book,
on pages 12, 21

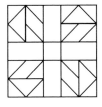

Jack in the Box
JM, p. 58
Found in this book,
on page 13

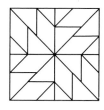

Diamond Jubilee
JM, p. 56
Found in this book,
on page 13

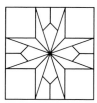

St. Louis Star
JB, p. 83
Found in this book,
on pages 15, 26, 28, 31,
51, 53, 64, 87, 103–7

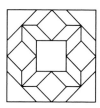

A Beauty
JB, p. 77
Found in this book,
on pages 15, 26–28, 49, 53,
63, 64, 87, 105–7

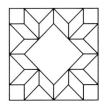

Ninepatch variation of
Michigan Beauty
BB #2538, p. 339
Found in this book,
on pages 16, 23, 157

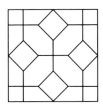

Designed by David Miller
Found in this book,
on pages 16, 21, 23, 157

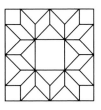

Mother's Choice
BB #2539b, p. 339
Found in this book,
on page 16

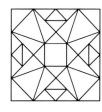

1904 Star
JB, p. 54
Found in this book,
on pages 17, 22, 26, 33–35,
42–44, 72, 102

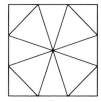

Octagons
BB #2704, p. 371
Found in this book,
on page 17

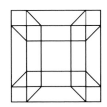

Rabbit's Paw
JM, p. 62
Found in this book,
on pages 19, 28

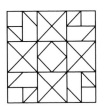

American Beauty
JM, p. 62
Found in this book,
on pages 19, 28

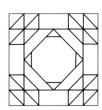

San Diego Sunshine
JM, p. 62
Found in this book,
on page 19

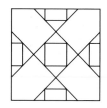

Home Treasure
JB, p. 53
Found in this book,
on pages 19–21, 30, 32

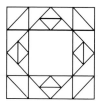

Variation of Flower Pot
JB, p. 57
Found in this book,
on pages 19, 20, 22, 26,
32, 33, 54–56

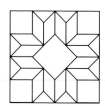

Michigan Beauty
JB, p. 58
Found in this book,
on pages 19, 26, 32, 103

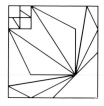

Variation of Magnolia Bud
BB #2208, p. 275
Found in this book,
on page 21

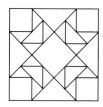

Double T
JB, p. 51
Found in this book,
on pages 26, 28, 33,
42–44, 48

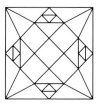

Washington Monument
JM, p. 59
Found in this book,
on page 27

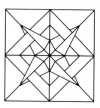

Mother's Day
JM, p. 62
Found in this book,
on pages 27, 28

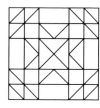

Spanish Moss
JM, p. 62
Found in this book,
on page 27

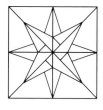

Manhattan Block
JM, p. 62
Found in this book,
on page 28

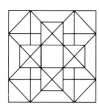

Grand Canyon Suite
JM, p. 60
Found in this book,
on page 28

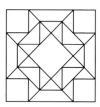

Valley of the Sun
JM, p. 60
Found in this book,
on pages 28, 52

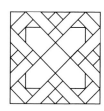

Chinatown
JM, p. 60
Found in this book,
on pages 28, 57

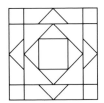

Cajun Spice
JM, p. 61
Found in this book,
on page 28

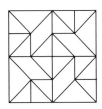

Pick of the Litter
SL4P, p. 26
Found in this book,
on page 28

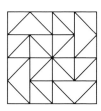

Ring around the Rosy
SL4P, p. 22
Found in this book,
on page 28

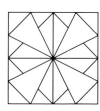

Keywest Beauty
SL4P, p. 29
Found in this book,
on pages 28, 48, 121–124

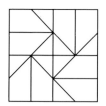

Happy Day
SL4P, p. 24
Found in this book,
on page 28

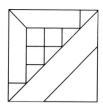

King's Crown
JB, p. 86
Found in this book,
on page 29

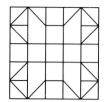

Double Wrench
JB, p. 88
Found in this book,
on pages 29, 102

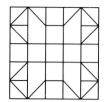

Sister's Choice
JB, p. 89
Found in this book,
on page 29

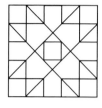

Providence Quilt Block
JB, p. 89
Found in this book,
on page 29

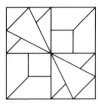

Prize Winner
SL4P, p. 30
Found in this book,
on page 30

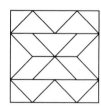

Dutchman's Puzzle
JB, p. 43
Found in this book,
on pages 42, 45–48

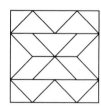

Double Z
JB, p. 46
Found in this book,
on page 48

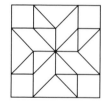

A Unique Design
JB, p. 46
Found in this book,
on page 48

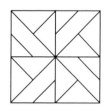

Wheels
JB, p. 43
Found in this book,
on page 48

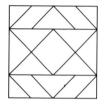

Mosaic, No. 22
JB, p. 75
Found in this book,
on page 48

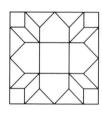

Weather Vane
JB, p. 78
Found in this book,
on pages 49, 51

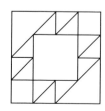

The Anvil
JB, p. 38
Found in this book,
on page 49

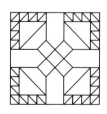

Uncle Sam's Favorite
JB, p. 92
Found in this book,
on page 49

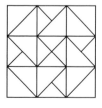

Card Trick
JB, p. 69 (designed by
Jeffrey Gutcheon, first
published in *The Perfect
Patchwork Primer,* 1973)
Found in this book,
on page 49

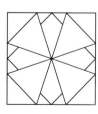

Nine-Patch Kaleidoscope
JB, p. 82 (designed by
Jinny Beyer, 1977)
Found in this book,
on page 49

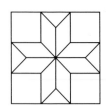

Godey Design
JB, p. 75
Found in this book,
on page 50

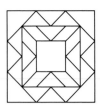

Double T
JB, p. 73
Found in this book,
on page 50

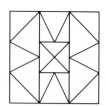

Double Z
JB, p. 71
Found in this book,
on page 50

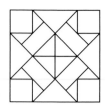

Octoberfest
JM, p. 60
Found in this book,
on pages 51, 52

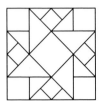

Home Grown
JM, p. 60
Found in this book,
on pages 51, 52

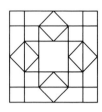

Hoosier Block
JM, p. 60
Found in this book,
on page 51

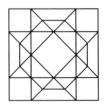

Georgetown Loop
JM, p. 60
Found in this book,
on pages 51, 57

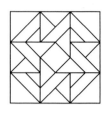

Land of the Midnight Sun
JM, p. 61
Found in this book,
on page 53

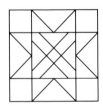

Independence Block
JM, p. 60
Found in this book,
on page 57

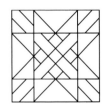

Royal Mile
JM, p. 60
Found in this book,
on page 57

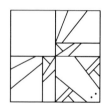

Frog Block
(origin unknown)
Found in this book,
on page 59

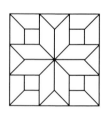

Boxes
JB, p. 75
Found in this book,
on page 87

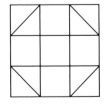

Shoo-Fly
JB, p. 64
Found in this book,
on pages 84, 105

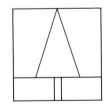

The Alpine Tree
CP, p. 37
Found in this book,
on page 89

Rose Wreath
(origin unknown)
Found in this book,
on page 89

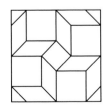

Building Blocks
JB, p. 81
Found in this book,
on pages 87, 103, 104

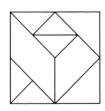

Unpublished block by
Michael James
Found in this book,
on pages 121–125

Bibliography

Bannister, Barbara, and Ford, Edna Paris. *The United States Patchwork Pattern Book.* New York: Dover Publications, 1976.

———. *State Capitals Quilt Blocks.* New York: Dover Publications, 1977.

Beyer, Jinny. *The Quilter's Album of Blocks & Borders.* McLean, Va.: EPM Publications, 1980.

Bezuszka, Stanley; Kenney, Margaret; and Silvey, Linda. *Designs from Mathematical Patterns.* Palo Alto, Calif.: Creative Publications, 1978.

Brackman, Barbara. *An Encyclopedia of Pieced Quilt Patterns.* Lawrence, Kans.: Prairie Flower Publishing, 1984.

Liby, Shirley. *Designing with Nine Patch.* Self-published, 812 W. Cromer, Muncie, Ind. 47303, 1987.

———. *Exploring Four Patch.* Self-published, 812 W. Cromer, Muncie, Ind. 47303, 1988.

Martin, Judy. *Judy Martin's Ultimate Book of Quilt Block Patterns.* Denver: Crosley-Griffith Publishing Company, 1988.

Palmer, Carolann. *Branching Out—Tree Quilts.* Bothell, Wash.: That Patchwork Place, 1986.

Waterman, V. Ann. *Design Your Own Repeat Patterns.* New York: Dover Publications, 1986.

Afterword

As I travel and teach, I usually stay with quiltmakers and their families rather than in hotels. Therefore, I am privy to some of the great wisdoms of the country—which I find affixed to the fronts of people's refrigerators. And I would like to end this book with a little saying that I found somewhere in my journeys, probably tacked up in someone's kitchen.

For those of you who find yourselves faint-hearted when it comes to reaching for the unexpected in your quilts, or are easily overwhelmed by everyone else's work at the quilt show or during the show-and-tell segment of your guild meeting, I pass on the following anonymous saying:

> Use the talents you possess.
> If only the best birds sang,
> The woods would be silent.

Information on "Reach for the Unexpected" lectures and workshops can be obtained by writing to the author at:

That Patchwork Place, Inc.
P.O. Box 118
Bothell, Washington 98041